The BUSINESS WOMEN'S WOW! FACTS

Dedication:

My inspiration comes from many. I start with my mom who died just as WOW! Facts was going to press. She was a lady who managed to mix both business and family in a magnificent way. With my dad, Les Fraser, Muriel Fraser established and built Casual Corner. She was an incredible business woman. In addition, this extraordinary woman possessed all the ideals that are right for business women of any time: Integrity, Dignity, Commitment and Loyalty.

I thank so many others, starting with the BWN team here on staff, and many others who have shared their friendship and intelligence and loyalty.

Edie Fraser, President, Business Women's Network

WOW! Facts Sponsors:
- AT&T
- AVIS
- BankBoston
- Career Center
- Forbes
- Legg Mason
- MacDonald Communications Corporation
- Staples
- Women's Business Journal
- WOWFactor

Compiled and edited by:
The Business Women's Network
Washington, DC

 Staff Salute

Congratulations to the members of the
Business Women's Network (BWN) staff.

From: Edie Fraser, President, Business Women's Network (BWN)
        Sandy Strzyzewski, COO, Business Women's Network (BWN)

Publisher:	Edie Fraser
Assistant Publisher:	Sandy Butler Whyte
Managing Editor:	Joanne Anderson
Editorial Director:	Donald Marzullo
Researchers:	Eve Scrogham
	Anais Sensiba
	Sarju Shrestha
	Chloe Arensberg
	Kimberly Vale
Editorial Staff:	Sandy Strzyzewski
	Rob Tompkins
	Gail Moore
	Paula McKenzie
Cover Design:	Rick Calendine
Production:	David Long
Technology and Web:	Tom DeShazo
Distribution:	Wanda DeLaRosa

ISBN #: 0-9656430-4-2
Available from 1-800-48-WOMEN or (202) 466-8209

TABLE OF CONTENTS

FACTS

© Business Women's Network, Washington, DC 20036
(800) 48-WOMEN
http://www.bwni.com

WOW!
FACTS

INTRODUCTION

A special publication of the Business Women's Network (BWN) — presenting thousands of facts on business women in a one-stop, easy reference tool.

WOW! Facts is the only compilation of facts about working women --- in its magnitude and scope --- covering the topics of interest about working women, entrepreneurs, the corporate world, the marketplace, diversity, awards and events. The facts, figures and examples showcase where working women are today and projects the outlook for tomorrow. This easy-to-use reference guide will prove to be an invaluable resource to both working women and companies interested in reaching the fast growing women's market. Its contents of facts, data, analyses and examples came from more than 550 resources, both public and private. Thousands of pages of information have been distilled, making this an indispensable reference guide.

WOW! Facts offers you a powerhouse of information, reflecting the energy, hard work and contributions by women to all sectors which are fueling the women's economic movement. WOW! Facts documents this phenomenon. The information is empowering and inspiring. Everyone will find facts of value and use. The facts are presented to inspire us all.

Thus, the apt name: **WOW!** Facts.

FACTS

Women across the United States are making a difference - in the workforce, in business ownership, in their communities and around the globe. Women are running their own businesses and are key to the growth of major corporations.

Women are a driving force in the U.S. economy with a purchasing power of $3 trillion. Women hold 11.1% of positions in boardrooms and the number is growing. *[Source: 1998 Census of Women Board of Directors of the Fortune 500, Catalyst 1999]* Women are fast becoming the majority of Internet users. Women hold the majority of investments. Women are responsible for balancing work-life challenges and are doing it admirably.

FACTS – MEETING A NEED

It is important for anyone involved in marketing, education, or business, and for women themselves, to better understand where working women and the women's marketplace are headed in the new millennium. That is why the Business Women's Network has created a special book with pertinent facts about this very subject: women. Where women stand in buying power … in politics … in the Boardroom … in technology … in the workforce … on investments … new business start-ups … health … and more.

 FACTS presents thousands of useful, easy to access facts for and about all these topics We have included resources throughout.

FACTS - Sources:

The Business Women's Network gives tribute and thanks to many organizations and government entities, including Catalyst, Inc., The National Foundation of Women Business Owners, *Working Woman* and *Working Mother* magazines, the National Women's Business Council, the

WOW!
FACTS

Small Business Administration, the U.S. Labor Department and hundreds or other organizations and institutions.
Don't guess. We'll tell you!

- Do you know which workforce gender will account for 58% of all those employed in the U.S. by year 2005 and which has been dropping in numbers?

- Do you know what the median income for married couple families was in 1997 where the wife was a salaried employee as opposed to her not working?

- Did you know that there are over 2,700 women's business associations and web sites where women can network, seek mentors, access educational support from their peers; where marketers can offer select products and services that add value to association memberships? And, do you know how to access them?

- If you were asked what percentage of all purchases are made by women (business and personal) in the U.S. today, what number would you anticipate that to be?

- Do you know the primary cause for 70% of businesses failing within their first three years of operation? Home office start-ups <u>do not</u> fall within this high fail rate.

- Did you know that 20% of all temporary workers are professionals, particularly in the accounting and technology fields?

- Would it surprise you to learn that, on average, the African-American female college graduate earns less than a white male high school graduate? Do you want to know if and how that is changing?

7

FACTS

- Did you know that only one in four employed care givers has access to elder-care resources and referral services through his or her employer – and that the majority of those elder-care givers are working women? Are you aware that in the mid-1990's only 38% of women retirees received pension benefits and 21% received health coverage that could be continued for life? Is this changing?

- Of the 1.1 million women-owned businesses owned by minorities by end of 1966, do you know which group reflected the largest growth rate, Asian-American, African-American or Hispanic-American? Do you know whether African-American entrepreneurs were the most likely to borrow capital to launch their firms? You'll be surprised by the answer and why.

- Do you know what age group is most responsible for new business start-ups in the U.S. today?

- Did you know Africa has ten million women entrepreneurs?

BWN's **WOW!** Facts gives hundreds of useful, easy-to access, facts for and about women. We include an extensive resource section on associations, educational and financial institutions, cities and states, child care and eldercare information sources and much more. Quick, easy to read and understand facts and figures are given. These pages are full of information on women in business, in technology, as entrepreneurs, on finance, health and diversity. Facts are included on accessing capital, climbing the corporate ladder, education, mentoring, work-life, politics, investments and more.

BWN acknowledges our corporate sponsors for their commitment to women and support of this project.

(the winning edge)

In business, as in life, success is often a matter of paying attention. Being awake to the opportunities around you. Being alert to new and better ways of doing things. Always being ready to learn and grow in your field.

And when it comes to your business, AT&T.ALL gives you the winning edge. It offers you a whole array of communications products and solutions designed to help you serve customers more efficiently, attract new ones and stay accessible, no matter where your hectic schedule takes you. And it's surprisingly simple – there's one easy to understand rate plan, one consolidated bill and just one number to call when you need assistance.

It's all within your reach.

So talk to your AT&T Account Executive, or call 1 888 288-9747 and let us help you put together the AT&T.ALL services best suited for your unique business needs.

Visit our Web site at http://www.att.com/attall
© 1998 AT&T

Women Entrepreneurs' Connection

The only banking program in New England dedicated to connecting women entrepreneurs with:

- **C**apital
  through our $1 Million Loan Initiative

- **I**nformation
  through our 1 888 BKB FOCUS #

- **A**dvocacy
  through our partnerships with national and local organizations

The National Foundation for Women Business Owners

Please visit our website for more information: www.bankboston.com

CareerCenter
www.bwni.com

BWN and JobOptions present their new online career center.

LEGG MASON Salutes Women of Yesterday, Today and Tomorrow.

Staples®
500 Staples Drive
farmington, MA 01701

February 25, 1999

Dear Business Women's Network:

Small business are growing at a pace four times faster than the growth of large businesses. Fully half of the households in the U.S. will have home offices by the Year 2000.

These statistics are a clear indication that small businesses and homeoffices are making their mark on American business in this decade and beyond. And, the growth of women-owned small businesses is helping to drive this pace. By focusing on entrepreneurs and homeoffice professionals in industries as diverse as computer technology, public relations, law and medicine, Staples is committed to serving the nation's women-owned businesses and homeoffice. Our goal is to take the cost and hassle our of running their business

As Staples tracks the needs of small business, it is everyday low prices for basic office supplies, new technology products and copy and computer services that clearly stand out as important for growing and sustaining a profitable small business.

We are dedicated to doing the very best we can to help the nation's women-owned small business grow and succeed in this exciting business climate.

Sincerely,

Jeanne Lewis
Executive Vice President, Marketing
Staples, Inc.

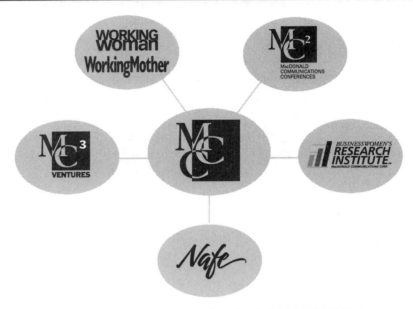

THE BUSINESS WOMEN'S NETWORK (BWN)

The Business Women's Network (BWN) has an expanded outreach to over 2,700 women's business associations and Web sites, and women business owners and organizations, not only in the United States, but also in Canada, Mexico, Western and Eastern Europe and Asia. We are working with more than 100 companies and 25 government entities. BWN has been sought out by U.S. government agencies, foreign governments, and associations to help build trade, to develop women's business and professional organizations, and to assist in creating association networks abroad.

The BWN infrastructure includes the following:

Number of Organizations and Web sites:
- In 1994, BWN had profiles of and relationships with 300 organizations.
- As of January 1999, BWN has a base of 2,700.
- By October 1999, the plan is to have 3,200.
- By September 2000 the plan is to increase the number to 4,000. This constituency represents over 10 million women.

U.S. Structure: State and Local:
BWN is establishing a grassroots network of state and local representatives for BWN - 100 by April 1999, 150 by fall 1999.

BWN International:
BWN has been working five years with groups on an international basis. In 1998 BWN included 100 Canadian organizations in its directory and an hosted delegations from Canada and Mexico at its Annual Conference. The October 1999 conference is expected to include delegates from 40 countries.

FACTS

Honorary Council: Representation of Corporate Women. The goal in 1998 was to close the year with 100 top women from Corporate America on our BWN Honorary Council. As of January 1999, there were 120 women in that group.

Advisory Council: Representation by leading women active in BWN. Each chairing a specific subcommittee.

Diversity Council: BWN's commitment is steadfast.
Resource Base:

Publications and Information – printed and electronic including:

- Business Women's Network Directory: Available in hard copy and online.
- Calendar of Women's Events – Available in hard copy and online. Includes data about more than 1,000 events for women to be held in the U.S. and around the world.
- The **WOW!** Facts. The most comprehensive compendium of economic facts and statistics on women available.

Annual Conference:

- BWN presents and annual conference with cutting edge issues; internationally-known speakers, and opportunities to network.
- The goal is to create more business for more women across more borders.
- For information call (800) 48 WOMEN, or register at our Web site www.BWNi.com.

18

FACTS

Systems for Communicating:

E-Mail: We have over 2,000 e-mail addresses from women's organizations. These can be leveraged as they help us reach millions women. Those include business owners, entrepreneurs, professional women, low income women, women's resource centers, and government agencies across the United States.

www.BWNi.com: Is the interactive Web site developed by BWN to convey publication information, current events, government procurement information and women's online resources and job options.

19

FACTS

CHAPTER 1: WORKING WOMEN

WOMEN IN THE WORKFORCE

WOW! Women make **up 48% of the U.S. workforce,** and the number is expected to **rise to 55% or higher by the year 2005**[1]. At the same time, the percentage of men in the workforce will have decreased by over 12%.

WOW! **The number of working women doubled** between 1970 and 1997, **from 30 million to 60 million**. By the year 2005, approximately **70 million women will work.**

WOW! **99% of women in the U.S. will work for pay at some point in their lives.**

WOW! Of the 60 million employed women in the U.S. in 1997, **44 million (74%) worked full-time** and **16 million (26%) worked part-time.**

WOW! Working women are working longer and harder than ever; an average of at least 5 hours more in 1998 than in 1977.

WOW! **Stress is the #1 problem for working women,** according to the U.S. Department of Labor.

---

[1] Exact numbers differ according to Labor, Census and Private studies.

© Business Women's Network, Washington, DC 20036
(800) 48-WOMEN
http://www.bwni.com

WOW! Between 1987 and 1997 **the number of women holding professional or managerial positions increased by 50%.**

PERCENT OF WOMEN AND MEN
WHO ARE IN THE WORK FORCE

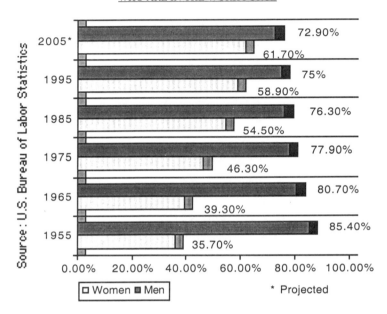

Source: U.S. Bureau of Labor Statistics

Year	Men	Women
2005*	72.90%	61.70%
1995	75%	58.90%
1985	76.30%	54.50%
1975	77.90%	46.30%
1965	80.70%	39.30%
1955	85.40%	35.70%

0.00% 20.00% 40.00% 60.00% 80.00% 100.00%

□ Women ■ Men   * Projected

WOW! **Proud To Work: 79% of women surveyed** by the U.S. Department of Labor **revealed their pride and satisfaction at being breadwinners for their families.**

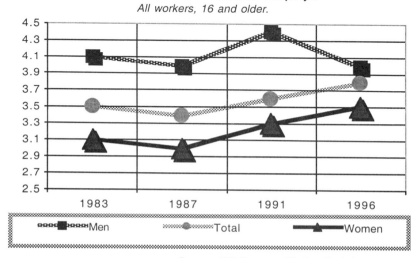

WOW! Women are staying longer at their jobs. Median tenure according to the Bureau of Labor Statistics **is approximately 3.8 years.**

Median Years with Current Employer
All workers, 16 and older.

	1983	1987	1991	1996
Men				
Total				
Women				

Source: US Bureau of Labor Satistics

WOW! Two-thirds of temporary workers are women.

WOW! The largest share of working women (41%) still work in technical and administrative support jobs and as sales clerks.

WOW! Where women work:

Service	48%
Wholesale or Retail Trade	21%
Manufacturing	12%
Finance, Insurance, Real Estate	9%
Public Administration	4%
Transportation, Communications, Public Utilities	4%
Agriculture	1%
Construction	1%
Mining	.04%

[Source: US Department of Labor]

WOW! 8% of women hold traditionally masculine jobs. 44% of women hold gender-neutral jobs.

WOW! 75% of health care jobs are held by women.

WOW! Women should consider careers in nontraditional occupations which are high-paying, says Ida Castro, Chairman of the U.S. Equal Employment Opportunity Commission. According to data from the Department of Labor's Women's Bureau, those high-paying, nontraditional careers include the following: mechanics, engineers, police detectives and firefighters.

WOW! Despite the increase in the number of working women, certain industries still overlook women. For example:

24

WOW! FACTS

1. **Only 8% of company sales representatives are women.**
2. **Only 17% of the insurance industry sales workforce is women.**
3. **Only 9% of engineers in the U.S. (about 2 million) are currently women,** an increase from 2% or 37,000 in 1976.

WOW! According to the U.S. Department of Labor, a big change occurred in the women's workforce over the fourteen-year period from 1983 to 1997. **In addition to increased numbers in the workforce, women are also holding a greater percentage of professional and managerial jobs.**

WOW! Women are balancing more demands than ever before while searching for ways to better their lives. Examples of resources to help them keep their lives in balance are: QuickBooks Women in Business Contest, (877) 213-7477, and Intuit's contest for women business owners, www.quickbooks.com.

WOMEN IN OCCUPATIONAL CATEGORIES
Trends Over a Fourteen Year Period

OCCUPATION	1983 % OF WORKFORCE	1997 % OF WORKFORCE	% INCREASE
Total workforce	43.7%	46.2%	2.5%
Executive/ Administrative	32.4%	44.3%	11.9%
Finance, Managers	38.6%	49.3%	10.7%
Personnel/Labor Relations Managers	43.9%	63.4%	19.5%
Purchasing Managers	23.6%	40.9%	17.3%
Managers: Marketing P.R./Advertising	21.8%	34.6%	12.8%
Managers (Health & Medicine)	57%	76.8%	19.8%
Accountants & Auditors	38.7%	56.6%	17.9%
Management Analysts	29.5%	42%	12.5%

[Source: U.S. Department of Labor Statistics]

WOW! 45% of employees are able to have flexible work schedules. 67% say they can take time off for family matters. 20% of employers report they permit employees to work at home. 37% offer job sharing. 61% provide part-time employment.

WOMEN IN THE PROFESSIONS
Trends Over a Fourteen Year Period

PROFESSION	1983 % OF WORKFORCE	1997 % OF WORKFORCE	% INCREASE
Professionals	48.1%	53.3%	5.2%
Architects	12.7%	17.9%	5.2%
Engineers	5.8%	9.6%	3.8%
Math/Computer	29.6%	30.4%	.8%
Natural Scientists	20.5%	31%	10.5%
Physicians	15.8%	26.2%	10.4%
Dentists	6.7%	17.3%	10.6%
Educators	36.3%	42.7%	6.4%
Economists	37.9%	52.2%	14.3%
Psychologists	57.1%	59.3%	2.2%
Lawyers	15.3%	26.6%	11.3%
Authors	46.7%	53.6%	6.9%

[Source: U.S. Department of Labor]

WORKING WIVES

WOW! The U.S. Bureau of Labor Statistics reports that in 1997, **60% of all marriages were dual-career marriages,** making up approximately 45% of the entire U.S. workforce.

WOW! Working wives contribute substantially to family incomes. In 1997, the **median income for married-couple families with the wife in**

27

the paid labor force was $60,669 compared with $36,027 for those without the wife in the paid labor force.

WOW! 10.2 million women earn more than their husbands.

WOW! Women Want to Work: 67% of married working women reported that they would continue to work even if there were no financial need to do so. *[Source: Two Careers, One Marriage: Making It Work in the Workplace, Catalyst 1998]*

WOW! 50% of ambitious women say that support from their husbands helps them succeed and 41% say their spouses make sacrifices.
[Source: Working Woman and Woman Trends]

WORKING MOTHERS

WOW! Dramatic increases have occurred in the numbers and percentages of mothers who worked during the past three decades. (Source: U.S Bureau of Labor Statistics)

WOW! 70% of all mothers are now employed, while in 1960 only 30% worked. This is an increase of more than 100%.

WOW! The percent of mothers who work while raising children between the ages of 6 and 18 has jumped from 54.9% in 1975, to 78.1% in 1997.

WOW! The increase in working mothers with children under the age of 6 has been even more dramatic, going from 39% in 1975, to 65% in 1997. 60% of mothers now return to work before a child is 1 year old.

WOW! **With two million children born to working mothers annually, a focus is clearly on such issues as parental leave and health care benefits.** Educational materials on these subjects are available from the Legal Defense and Education Fund and the U.S. Department of Labor.

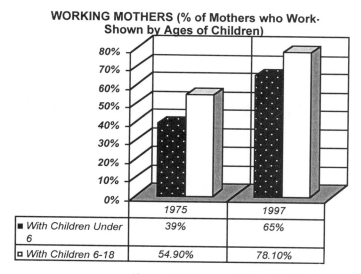

	1975	1997
■ With Children Under 6	39%	65%
◻ With Children 6-18	54.90%	78.10%

[Source: US Bureau of Labor Statistics]

WOW! **Nearly 1 in 5 employed parents are single; 73% of these single working parents are women,** and 27% are men.

FACTS

 The **100 Best Companies for Working Mothers** as selected by
Working Mother Magazine's Annual Survey, October, 1998

ACACIA	AETNA
Allstate	American Express
American Home Products	AMOCO
AT&T	Autodesk
Bankers Trust	Bank of America
Bausch & Lomb	Bayfront Medical Center
BP Exploration (Alaska)	Bristol-Myers Squibb
Chase Manhattan Bank	Chrysler
Cigna	Cinergy
Citicorp/Citibank	Commercial Financial Services
Coopers & Lybrand	Corning
Dayton Hudson	Deloitte & Touche
Donaldson, Lufkin & Jenrette	Dupont
Dupont Pharmaceuticals	Eastman Kodak
Ernst & Young	Fannie Mae
Federal Express	First Chicago NBD
First Tennessee Bank	First Union
Gannett	General Mills
Glaxo Wellcome	GTE
Hallmark	Hewlett-Packard
Hill, Holliday, Connors, Cosmopulos	Hoffmann-La Roche
IBM	Imation
JFK Medical Center	Johnson & Johnson
Life Technologies	Eli Lilly
Lincoln Financial Group	Lotus Development
Lucent Technologies	Marriott International
MassMutual	Mattel
MBNA America Bank	Mentor Graphics
Merck	Merrill Lynch
Millipore	J.P. Morgan
Neuville Industries	Northern Trust
Patagonia	Pfizer Phoenix Home Life
Price Waterhouse	Principal Financial Group
Proctor & Gamble	Prudential
Rex Healthcare	Ridgeview
Rockwell	Saint Luke's Hospital of Kansas City

S.C. Johnson & Son	KPMG
Sara Lee	SAS Institute
Sequent Computer Systems	SNET (Southern New England Telecom)
Stride Rite	Texas Instruments
The Benjamin Group	Beth Israel Deaconess Medical Center
The Bureau of National Affairs	Calvert Group
The Seattle Times	Security Benefit Group
The St. Paul Companies	Salt River Project
The Vanguard Group	Warner-Lambert
Tom's of Maine	TRW
Turner Broadcasting System	Union Pacific Resources Group
Universal Studios	UNUM Life Insurance
UPMC Health System	USAA
Xerox	

WOW! 65% of women in senior management positions have children, and 73% of these mothers are raising children under the age of 18, and 85% of executive women employ domestic help. *[Source: Women in Corporate Leadership: Progress and Prospects, Catalyst, 1996]*

WOW! 90% of women with children say they are "ambitious." *[Source: Adelphi University Study]*

WOW! Working mothers hold half of all professional and managerial positions.

WOW! Women with children at home are more stressed and had higher levels of the "distress" hormone cortisol than women without children at home, according to a study published in *Psychosomatic Medicine*.

WOW! A Harvard Business School Survey shows that more working mothers with children have higher incomes, a reversal of earlier trends.

INFLUENTIAL WORKING MOTHERS

WOW! Every year *Working Mother Magazine* identifies the "25 Most Influential Working Mothers." The most recent list, presented features the Senior Vice President of a major children's book publisher; the founder and designer of a major fashion house; a major investment banker; and Atlanta's Police Chief. W*orking Mother Magazine* found that women with children are emerging as powerful leaders in such competitive fields as sports, the food and wine industry, academic medicine and investment banking.

WOW! The 25 Most Influential Working Mothers – January 1999

[*Source: Working Mother Magazine, December 1998*]

1	Jean Feiwel, 45, Senior Vice President, Publisher and Editor-in-Chief of Scholastic Books, mother of one daughter;
2	Linda Mason, 44, Chairman of Bright Horizons Family Solutions, mother of two daughters and one son;
3	Dana Buchman, 47, Founder & Designer of Dana Buchman, mother of two daughters;
4	Andrea Immer, 32, Master Sommelier and Beverage Director for B.E. Group, mother of one son;
5	Patricia Fili-Krushel, 45, President of ABC Television Network, mother of one daughter and one son;
6	Renee Fleming, 39, Lyric Soprano, mother of two daughters;
7	Lois Gibbs, 47, Environmental Activist, mother of three sons and one daughter;
8	Jill Greenthal, 42, Investment Banker for Donaldson, Lufkin & Jenrette (DLJ), mother of one daughter and one son;
9	Marcy Whitebook, 50, Founder and Co-Director of the Center for the Child Care Workforce, mother of one son;
10	Beverly J. Harvard, 47, Police Chief in Atlanta, mother of one daughter;

11	**Bernadine Healy, M.D., 54, Dean of the College of Medicine and Public Health at Ohio State University,** mother of two daughters;
12	**JoAnn Heffernan Heisen, 48, Member of the Executive Committee and Worldwide Vice President and Chief Information Officer for Johnson & Johnson,** mother of two sons and two daughters;
13	**Antonia Hernandez, 50, President and General Counsel of the Mexican American Legal Defense and Education Fund,** mother of two sons and a daughter;
14	**Cynthia Hess, 42, General Manager ,Small Car Platform Engineering for Chrysler Corporation,** mother of two sons;
15	**Prema Mathai-Davis, 48, CEO of YMCA of the USA,** mother of twin daughters and one son;
16	**Shirley A. Jackson, 52, Chairman of the US Nuclear Regulatory Commission (NRC),** mother of one son;
17	**Maya Lin, 39, Architect and Designer,** mother of one daughter;
18	**Martha McClintock, 51, Professor of Psychology at The University of Chicago,** mother of one daughter and one son;
19	**Ann S. Moore, 48, President of People Magazine,** mother of one son;
20	**Anna Quindlen, 46, Author and Social Critic,** mother of two sons and one daughter;
21	**Laura Scher, 39, CEO of Working Assets,** mother of one daughter;
22	**Susan B. Thistlewaite, 50, President, The Chicago Theological Seminary,** mother of three sons;
23	**Laura D'Andrea Tyson, 51, Dean of the Walter A. Haas School of Business at the University of California, Berkeley,** mother of one son;
24	**Phyllis Yale, 41, Managing Director of Bain & Company,** mother of two daughters;
25	**Val Ackerman, 39, President of the Women's National Basketball Association,** mother of two daughters.

SALARIES OF WOMEN WITH MBA'S AND CHILDREN

Class of 1973	Class of 1983
53% were mothers	70% were mothers
Income was less with children	Income was more with children
Income with **$116,714**	Income w/o **$299,900**

Note: The survey was responded to by 101 graduate students. The **average income of those working was $183,800 and 7 of them made over $1 million.**

CHILD CARE

WOW! 56% of women with children age five and under state that finding affordable child care is a serious problem.

WOW! 66% of workers today find it relatively easy to take time off during the workday to address family/personal matters; yet **only 50% of employed parents are able to take a few days off to care for sick children without losing pay.**

WOW! Good child care provided in high-quality centers results in better social development and language development for children according to the Center for the Childcare Workforce. However, the average salaries for teachers at **child care centers in the US have risen very little in the last 10 years** and range from only $13,000 to $19,000. Teaching assistants fare even worse, with average salaries between $10,000 and $12,000 below the official poverty level for a family of three.

WOW! Women entrepreneurs have directly involved themselves in bettering the situation of the working mother by establishing such organizations as Bright Horizons Family Solutions, the Center for the Child Care Workforce and Lipton Childcare.

WOW! Family and childcare centers are developing in every community. *Working Mother* (April, 1999,) cited the NOVA Southeastern University in Tampa, Florida's Family Center and its innovative day care program.

WOW! Ten Best States for Child Care according to *Working Mother Magazine*, January 1998:

- California
- Connecticut
- Maryland
- Minnesota
- Washington

- Colorado
- Hawaii
- Massachusetts
- Vermont
- Wisconsin

Criteria Used by *Working Woman* for Choosing 10 Best States for Childcare:

Quality: includes accredited centers; accredited family child care; child-to-adult ratios; group size; caregiver training; caregiver pay.

FACTS

Safety: adult supervision; size at which family care is regulated; playground surfaces; hand washing and inspections.

Availability: tax breaks and child care tax credit; resources and referrals; public pre-K; pay rate.

Commitment: actions taken by state officials to improve and expand child care from current levels. "The Governor and/or state legislators had to make child care a high priority on the state agenda by pushing for policies to improve its quality and expand its supply." *[Source: Working Mother, July-August 1998]*

WOW! The Department of Labor announces the Business to Business Mentoring Initiative on Childcare. President Clinton and Labor Secretary, Alexis Herman announced this initiative to help with problems created by the fact that approximately 30 million U.S. families have children under the age of 14. In 1997, there were 14.6 million households where both parents worked, and 4.7 million single parent households. The mentoring program has been established to "meet the needs for this millennium. For information contact the Women's Bureau of the Department of Labor (202) 219-6611 or www.dol.gov/dol/wb

36

WOW! RESOURCES FOR BACKUP CHILD CARE[2]

Examples:

- **AMERICAN BUSINESS COLLABORATION FOR QUALITY DEPENDENT CARE**: Consortium of corporations such as Prudential, AETNA, IBM, and AT&T working for child and elderly care.
- **BRIGHT HORIZONS:** Builds and operates full-time and back-up child care centers nationwide for both corporations and communities. Based in Cambridge, Massachusetts, (800) 324-4386.
- **CAREGIVERS ON CALL**: An emergency in-home dependent care program for corporations. The company subcontracts with existing home health agencies. Based in New York, (800) 225-1200.
- **CHILD CARE AWARE:** A national information help line that can refer you to resources in your area. (800) 424-2246
- **CHILDREN'S WORLD LEARNING CENTERS:** Owns and operates a national chain of child care centers; sells slots to companies. Based in Golden, Colorado, (303) 526-3252.
- **CHILDRENFIRST, INC**: Designs, develops and operates dedicated backup centers for single companies and consortiums of companies nationwide. Based in Boston, (617) 330-8687.
- **CORPORATE FAMILY SOLUTIONS:** A national work-family firm that helps corporations set up and operate backup and full-service child care programs. Based in Nashville, Tennessee. (800) 452-2111.
- **KINDERCARE LEARNING CENTERS, INC:** Owns and operates a national chain of child care centers; offers drop-in care at many locations. Based in Portland, Oregon, or (877)-KINDERCARE, www.kindercare.com.
- **LIPTON CORPORATE CHILD CARE CENTERS, INC**: Owns and operates a national chain of backup child care centers and sells slots to companies. Based in Washington, D.C., (202) 416-6875.

---

[2] Note: There are many more day care resources at the local level.

FACTS

WOW! The Families and Work Institute, a non-profit New York research group, surveyed some 1,000 employees to determine what types of child care services and support they offer parents. The results are shown in chart below.

Service Offered	% of Companies
Offer some type of child-care program	9%
Help workers pay for child care	5%
Provide backup of emergency care for workers' kids when other arrangements fail	4%
Reimburse employees for child-care costs when they work late	4%
Provide access to information to help locate child-care in the community	36%

WOW! Caring for Kids: Lifetime's Commitment marks a comprehensive plan to use electronic media and cyberspace to give women the opportunity to participate in the national debate on childcare. Lifetime Television for Women has arranged on its Web site (www.lifetimetv.com) for women and families to share information on childcare. The coalition of advocacy organizations is impressive as they join Lifetime in the Caring for Kids Advocacy.

CARING FOR PARENTS

WOW! One of five working parents is part of what is called the **"sandwich generation,"** because they are simultaneously raising children and caring for elderly parents.

WOW! **70% of working women are caregivers for elderly parents.**

WOW! Only **one in four employed caregivers for the elderly has access to eldercare resources and referral services through his or her employer.**

WOW! **Families involved in eldercare in the U.S. spend about $2 billion total per month of their own money.**

WOMEN AND RETIREMENT

WOW! **AMERICA IS AGING**
- Today, some **40 million Americans are 60 or older.**
- The number **of people age 50-65 will increase at twice the rate** of the overall population.
- **One out of every nine baby boomers will live at least to age 90.**
  [Source: Women In Business, July/August 1998]

WOW! The Bureau of Labor Statistics estimates that by the year **2000,** only **39% of the work force will be under the age 35.**

WOW! The Federal Reserve Board found that women are as likely to take risks as men when investing for retirement.

WOW! Data from the Pension and Welfare Benefits Administration of the U.S. Department of Labor reveals that in **1994, only 38% of women retirees received pension benefits and only 21% received health coverage that could be continued for life.**

WOW! Among the **elderly poor, 75% are women; 80% of this group** were not poor before they were widowed.

WOW! Inflation is expected to double in the next 18 years, thereby reducing the value of retirement savings, for men and women alike.

WOW! Effective in the year 2000, **the age for collecting full Social Security benefits will gradually rise until it reaches 67** for people born in 1960 or later.

WOW! According to a Yankelovich poll, **the word "stressful" is used more frequently to describe the '90s than any other word - particularly by older women.**

CHAPTER 2: THE WOMEN'S MARKET

WOW! Consumer spending by women amounts to **$3.3 trillion per year.**

WOW! **The purchasing power and economic clout of women is growing exponentially** as the number of working women rises, and they move into higher paying jobs.

WOW! **Women purchase 81% of all products and services, both business and consumer, thus impacting trillions of dollars of sales.**

WOW! **80% of all checks written in the U.S. are signed by women.**

WOW! **The purchase rate of women of color is high** in today's market. Over all, **African-American, Asian-American and Hispanic-American households have surpassed white households in per capita spending. The spending by women of color** was estimated to be **more than $500 billion in 1997.**

WOW! **The purchasing power of Hispanic Americans was $348 billion nationwide in 1997**, a 50% increase from 5 years earlier.
Note: For more data on spending by minorities, see Chapter 17, Diversity.

FACTS

WOMEN BUYING FOR FAMILIES

WOW! 75% of all household finances are handled by women. 53% of all family investment decisions are made by women.

WOW! Women make 75% of all healthcare decisions for U.S. households.

WOW! Women make **81% of all retail purchases and buy 82% of all** groceries.

WOW! Women are the primary travel planners in approximately **75% of all households** nationwide, spending more than $188 billion on leisure and travel, **and $26.1 billion on domestic air travel annually.**

AUTOMOTIVE PURCHASES

WOW! Women influence 85% of all car purchases.

WOW! Women **account for some 50% of all vehicle purchases** (sources vary on exact percentage) and are expected to account **for at least 60% of purchases by the year 2005.**

WOW! More than 65% of customers who take vehicles to a repair shop are women.

42

WOW! **Two-thirds of the women** in the U.S. say they **dislike the car buying process**. In addition, **81% say they are not treated with respect when they purchase cars.** Approximately **60% of women distrust car salespeople.** (This supercedes the distrust of lawyers and congressional representatives, which are 41% and 44% respectively.)

WOW! Despite the increasing number of women in the general workforce, and the percentage of women auto buyers, **the number of female auto sales-personnel remains very low (8%).**

WOMEN BUYING FOR BUSINESSES

WOW! Women in business will invest **$44.5 billion in high technology office products this year** and billions more for office supplies.

WOW! **Women comprise 53% of all purchasing agents in corporations.**

WOW! **Women business travelers now account for 50% of all trips,** spending approximately **$175 billion on 14 million business trips annually.**

TRAVEL AND HOSPITALITY

WOW! Because women make up more than 50% of the business travel business and plan 75% of family travel **airlines, hotels and travel**

43

companies are now specifically targeting the woman traveler with special services and marketing efforts. For example, **Royal Caribbean Lines offers a special program for women in business at sea.**

WOW! Women business travelers say they want the following from a hotel:
- A home away from home;
- A place to bring kids;
- Security, and;
- Exercise facilities.

INTERNET BUYING

WOW! Purchasing goods on the Internet is the hottest new trend in the economy.

WOW! Sales on the Internet reached almost $2.4 billion in 1997 and will climb by billions later in 1999. **Women represent only 35% of E-commerce to date.** However, **that number is expected to rise to 40% by the year 2000** and to **50% by the year 2005.**

WOW! Overall Electronic Commerce:
- **1998:** Online shopping accounted for $7 billion in sales, a 300% increase from 1997.
- **2000:** Online shopping should reach **$10 billion in sales.**

WOW! Women on the Internet are expected to spend $3.5 billion on technology by the year 2000.

WOW! A survey of Internet shoppers was conducted in **November/December 1998** by Bruskiln/Goldring Research for Clinique. Data included the following:

- **The percentage of women with Internet access who have purchased online (35%) was almost exactly the same as the percentage of men (37%) making purchases.**
- White women shoppers tended to purchase basic items and buy in greater quantities than men.
- **The highest percentage of women shoppers (18%) spent between $100 and $200,** while the highest percentage of male shoppers (36%) only spent $25 to $50.

45

© Business Women's Network, Washington, DC 20036
(800) 48-WOMEN
http://www.bwni.com

WOW! FACTS™

FACTS

CHAPTER 3: ENTREPRENEURSHIP

WOMEN BUSINESS OWNERS

WOW! There are now **8.5 million women-owned businesses in the U.S.**, up from **6.4 million in 1992**.

WOW! These **women-owned businesses make up about 38% of all businesses** in the U.S.

WOW! By the **year 2000, 40% of all U.S. businesses** will be owned by women, and by 2005, that number will rise to approximately 50%. *[Source: BWN]*

WOW! **Women-owned businesses are growing faster than the overall economy** in each of the top 50 metropolitan areas of the U.S., with a 43% increase compared to the 26% for all businesses.

WOW! **Women entrepreneurs are starting new companies at twice the rate of men, thus significantly increasing the growth rate of new businesses.**

WOW! **Women-owned businesses** in the U.S. **generated $3.1 trillion in revenue in 1997**. According to the U.S. Small Business Administration, this figure rose almost **100% in five years**, from the 1992 level of $1.6 trillion.

47

WOW! **Women-owned businesses employed more than 23.7 million people in 1997**. This was a 262% increase in employees from 1987. The employment rolls for women owned businesses are expected to reach 28 million by the end of 1999.

WOW! **The combined total number of employees of women-owned businesses is 25% more than the total number of employees of all the Fortune 500 companies worldwide combined and accounts for some 25% of all U.S. employees.**

WOW! **The largest share of women-owned firms (59.1%) are in the service and sales sectors.**

WOW! **New companies headed by women stay in business longer than the average U.S. company.**

WOW! **39% of women business leaders** recently surveyed by The National Foundation for Women Business Owners **are involved in the international marketplace**; 47% of that number became involved just last year.

WOW! There will be **4.7 million self-employed women in the U.S. by 2005**, an increase of 77% since 1983.

WOW! **Top metropolitan areas for women-owned businesses ranked by number of firms, sales and employment** in 1996 were: (1) New York,

NY; (2) Los Angeles-Long Beach, CA; (3) Chicago, IL; (4) Philadelphia, PA-NJ; (5) Washington, DC-MD-VA-WV; (6) Houston, TX; (7) Seattle-Bellevue-Everett, WA; (8) Nassau-Suffolk, NY; (9) Detroit, MI; (10) Orange County, CA; and (11) Dallas, TX. These areas are holding their rankings.

WOW! **Cities with the fastest growth in women-owned businesses** (employment and sales) are: (1) Portland, OR (2) Seattle-Bellevue-Everett, WA; (3) Phoenix-Mesa, AZ; (4) Houston, TX; (5) Nashville, TN; (6) Miami, FL; and (7) Sacramento, CA.

WOW! **Why entrepreneurship? 51% of women business owners with prior private sector experience cite the desire for more flexibility as the major reason for leaving their corporate positions. Another 29% cite "glass ceiling"** issues as a key reason for their move to entrepreneurship.

WOW! **Women choose new paths more often than their male counterparts,** especially given the strong growth of the U.S. economy. While 60% of male business owners stay within the fields worked in previously, **more than 50% of women choose to pursue new directions.**

WOW! **Being laid off by a company is not a major reason why people turn to entrepreneurship.** In fact, 93% of laid-off managers who were surveyed by the Chicago placement firm Challenger, Gray & Christmas, found a job with another company and most did so within 4 months.

WOW! FACTS

WOW! **60% of all women business owners** surveyed said that despite difficult times they **would choose business ownership again if they were to have the choice to do it over.**

WOW! **Younger people are important contributors to new businesses. Those under 30**, according to the National Federation of Independent Business (NFIB), **are responsible for 32% of new business startups.** Some **50% of new business owners got started in their ventures before reaching the age of 35.**

WOW! **The role of women in family-run businesses is increasing for the first time.** Currently, only 5% are run by women. However, **25% of those family firms surveyed by the Center for Family Business in 1998** said that they are **likely to appoint a woman as the next CEO.**

WOW! The <u>Top 500 Women Entrepreneurs</u> – 1998
- **Total revenues of the 500 were $71.7 billion.**
- Total number of **employees were 326,053.**
- **Fastest growing fields**: construction, transportation, agriculture and manufacturing.

WOW! The **Working Woman 500 Conference** is held annually. Information is available at (888) 735-6192 or at <u>www.workingwomanmag.com</u>.

50

FACTS

WOW! According to *Working Woman Magazine*, the Top 50 Women Entrepreneurs for the year 1998 were:

1)	JM Family Enterprises	Pat Moran
2)	Fidelity Investments	Abigail Johnson
3)	Ingram Industries	Martha Ingram
4)	Carlson Companies	Marilyn Carlson
5)	Little Caesar Enterprises	Marian Ilitch
6)	Mary Kay Cosmetics	Mary Kay Ash
7)	Raley's	Joyce Raley Teal
8)	The Washington Post Co.	Katharine Graham
9)	Alberto-Culver Co.	Bernice Lavin/Carol Bernick
10)	84 Lumber	Maggie Hardy Magerko
11)	Roll International	Lynda Resnick
12)	Warnaco Group	Linda Wachner
13)	Frank Consolidated Enter.	Elaine S. Frank
14)	Axel Johnson Group	Antonia Axson Johnson
15)	Cumberland Farms	Lily Bentas
16)	Sutherland Lumber	Donna Sutherland Pearson
17)	Minyard Food Stores	Liz Minyard/Gretchen Williams
18)	Printpack	Gay Love
19)	Software Spectrum	Judy Sims
20)	J. Crew	Emily Woods
21)	Donna Karan International	Donna Karan
22)	ASI (Asia Source Inc.,)	Christine Liang
23)	PC Connection	Patricia Gallup
24)	Jockey International	Donna Steigerwaldt
25)	Johnson Bros. Wholesale Liquor	Lynn Johnson
26)	Rodale Press	Ardath Rodale
27)	The Copley Press	Helen Copley
28)	Gear Holdings	Bettye Martin Mushan
29)	The Pampered Chef	Doris Christopher
30)	Troy Motors	Irma Elder

51

31) Tootsie Roll Industries	Ellen Gordon
32) US Gas Transportation	Nanci Mackenzie
33) Commercial Financial Services	Kathyrn Bartmann
34) Chas. Levy Companies	Barbara Levy Kipper
35) Jenny Craig International	Jenny Craig
36) Syms Corp.	Marcy Syms
37) Oshman's Sporting Goods	Marilyn Oshman
38) Columbia Sportswear	Gertrude Boyle
39) Westfall-O'Dell Trans. Services	Jane O'Dell
40) The Lundy Packaging Company	Annabelle Fetterman
41) TLC Beatrice International	Loida Nicolas Lewis
42) Johnson Publishing Co.	Linda Johnson Rice
43) Authentic Fitness Corp.	Linda J. Wachner
44) Smead Manufacturing	Ebba Hoffman/Sharon Avent
45) O'Reilly Automotive	Rosalie Wooten
46) Logistix	Marta Weinstein
47) Pleasant Company	Pleasant Rowland
48) J&R Music and Computer World	Rachelle Friedman
49) Rose Acre Farms	Lois Rust
50) Sun Coast Resources	Lathy Prasnick Lehne

[Source: Working Woman Magazine, May 1998]

WOW! **Recognition is important.** As Working Woman holds its annual Top 500 Awards, it also sponsors with BankOne Entrepreneurial Excellence Awards.

WOW! Business owners are increasingly eager to see themselves and their company on a list of "Top Entrepreneurs." Many such lists are developed annually by publications and business centers across the country. The following list cites many "sponsors" of such lists:

Area	Sponsor	Deadline
Atlanta, GA	*Atlanta Business Journal*	April
Austin, TX	*Austin Business Journal*	July
Charlotte, NC	*Charlotte Business Journa*	lJuly
Columbus, OH	*Business First of Columbus*	August
Dallas. TX	*Dallas Business Journal*	August
Denver, CO	*Denver Business Journal*	March
Houston, TX	*University of Houston SBDC*	June
Hawaii	*Pacific Business News*	April
Jacksonville, FL	*Jacksonville Business Journal*	May
Orlando, FL	*Orlando Business Journal*	June
Phoenix, AZ	*The Business Journal*	August
Philadelphia. PA	*Wharton SBDC*	July
Pittsburgh, PA	*Pittsburgh Business Times*	July
Portland, OR	*The Business Journal*	April
Raleigh, NC	*Triangle Business Journal*	July
Sacramento, CA	*Sacramento Business Journal*	April
San Francisco,CA	*San Francisco Business Times*	August
San Jose, CA	*San Jose Business Journal*	July
Puget Sound,WA	*Puget Sound Business Journal*	August
Washington, DC	*Washington Business Journal*	May

53

FACTS

Women's Business, Boston

Women's Business is designed to meet the needs and interests of today's professional and it celebrates the phenomenal growth and success women are achieving in a variety of arenas. It provides information that working women need to develop and grow in their businesses. And, most importantly, it offers the opportunity for women to get the visibility they need and deserve. As a resource and mentor. It is also the place where men can read about the exciting accomplishments women in business are achieving. Women's Business is published monthly by Vicki Donlan in Boston, MA and is circulated to 25,000 in Massachusetts, southern New Hampshire, and Rhode Island. Subscriptions are available at $39.00 per year. For more information www.womensbiz.com

Women Entrepreneurs, Dallas

Women Entrepreneurs chronicles the growth and success of women in business in Texas. First published in 1992, it is a monthly publication with a circulation 30,000. It is published by Diversity Publishing and edited by Judy Jones. This publication serves as an advocate as well as a resource for women in business and provides helpful business and career building ideas every month. Women Entrepreneurs provides a communications link to the influential group of women executives and entrepreneurs. If the women's business market is of interest to you then Women Entrepreneurs is your indispensable guide. Subscriptions are $12 per year, to subcribe please call 214-369-9393. www.womens-enterprise.com

Women's Business Journal, South Florida and National

The first national newspaper written exclusively for and about women in business. Unlike mainstream business press, the publication identifies and publishes news and information on the issues of interest to women in business, as well as profiles of the women who are leading the way to success in the business world. Since its launch in 1996, the paper has grown from an initial print run of 25,000 in South Florida to a over 100,000 papers distributed regionally and nationally each month. Cover stories and topics planned for 1999 include: Women and Money, Women

54

Entrepreneurs, Reinventing Feminism, Women and Power, The Female Side of Competition and The Male/Female Balance.

Women's Business Chronicle Denver, **Colorado**

Women's Business Chronicle is dedicated to professional women who want, need and deserve in-depth business news and information. Women business owners and professional women are the readership of Women's Business Chronicle. This paper brings news, stories and features that will lead women to success. This newspaper is intended to be a clearinghouse of information and resources that will never compromise its editorial integrity of content. *Women's Business Chronicle* is the women's business community newspaper intended to inspire, inform and educate. The mission of the newspaper is to provide women professionals and women business owners with information and news that will enable them to grow successful businesses and to provide access to resources that will position professional women for success.

MINORITY WOMEN ENTREPRENEURS

WOW! From 1987 to 1996, **the number of women-owned businesses owned by minorities rose by 153% to nearly 1.1 million.** (Hispanic-American: rose 206% to 384,000; Asian/Native-American: rose 138% to 305,700; and African-American: rose 135% to 405,200.)

WOW! One in eight of the nearly eight million women-owned **businesses in the U.S. – 1,067,000 enterprises – are owned by a women of color.**

WOW! 13% of the total number **of women-owned businesses in the U.S. are owned by minority women.**

55

WOW! **African-American entrepreneurs were the least likely to borrow capital to launch their firms** (29%), compared to Asian-American (37%), Native/Alaska-American (45%), Caucasian (49%), and Hispanic-American (51%) women business owners.

WOW! **Women-owned firms grew at double the overall business** growth rate in the U.S. during the past decade, and **minority-owned firms** grew at triple the national rate, according to 1997 National Foundation for Women Business Owners report.

Most Women, Regardless of Color, are Motivated to Entrepreneurship to Improve Their Situation and Gain Control

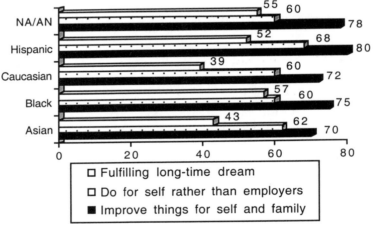

[Note: NA/AN = Native American/Alaska Native]
[Source: National Foundation for Women Business Owners and AT&T]

56

WOW! 52% of black women business owners had mentors when starting their business.

WOW! The majority of **black women start their businesses alone** and they are more likely than other minority groups to start one **related to their former career.**

WOW! 5 Firms in the 1998 *Black Enterprise* Industrial Service 100 list are headed by women.
- TLC Beatrice International Holdings Inc.
- Soft Sheen Products Inc.
- Madison Inc.
- V&J Foods
- Management Technology Inc.

WOW! 3 Auto Dealers on the *Black Enterprise* Auto Dealer 100 list have women CEO's.
- Bob Ross Buick Inc.
- Rodgers Chevrolet
- Huntsville Dodge

WOW! 2 Advertising Agencies on the *Black Enterprise* 100 list for Advertising have Women CEO's.
1. Carol H. Williams
2. Caroline Jones Inc.

57

FACTS

WOW! On the Black Enterprise 100 list for Banks, 4 have women CEO's.

- Mechanics & Farmers Bank
- Illinois Service Federal S&L Association
- United Bank of Philadelphia
- People's National Bank of Commerce

FACTS

FINANCE FOR ENTREPRENEURS

WOW! **Access to capital and credit are the top concerns of women who want to start a business.** How do these women finance businesses? The barriers are real, but a creative approach has made business ownership a reality for many women. Arming themselves with information on how bankers make decisions is a strategic way to go about getting funding.

WOW! Some **52% of women had traditional bank credit in 1998**, an increase of just 5% in just two years. **60% used a nontraditional source** (finance company, personal credit card, etc), according to the National Foundation of Women Business Owners (NFWBO).

WOW! **The amount of credit available to women business owners has also increased.** 33% had $50,000 or more in 1998 compared to the 20% having access to that amount in 1996.

WOW! **Women business owners** still have significantly **less bank credit** than **men business owners.** More than 60% of men had bank credit in 1998, and they also had more credit on average than women.

WOW! In 1998 **more than twice as many men as women had credit in the categories of $100,000 to $499,000 and over $500,000.**

59

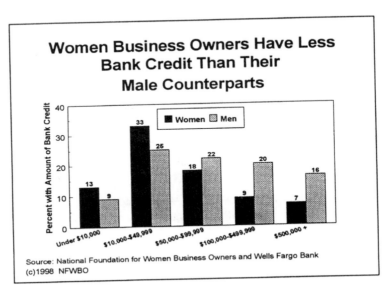

Women Business Owners Have Less Bank Credit Than Their Male Counterparts

WOW! When it comes to obtaining bank credit, women of color fare significantly worse than do Caucasian women.

Almost twice as many Caucasian women business owners have bank credit, when compared with their black counterparts (60% versus 38%).

WOW! Hispanic-American, Asian-American, and Native- American women have less bank credit than Caucasian women, but more than African-American women business owners, with 50%, 45%, and 42% respectively.

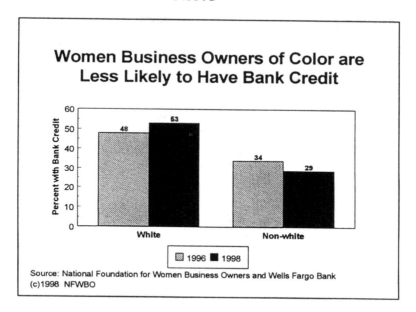

Women Business Owners of Color are Less Likely to Have Bank Credit

Source: National Foundation for Women Business Owners and Wells Fargo Bank
(c)1998 NFWBO

WOW! 33% of women business owners perceive some degree of gender-based discrimination from their financial institutions.

WOW! The three **biggest complaints from women entrepreneurs regarding their working relationships with banks to obtain financing** are:

- The banks ask for greater collateral from women than from men;
- Women are asked to provide more assets than men; and
- A limited track record is viewed with bias by the banks.

61

WOW! Almost 79% of women-owned businesses had access to credit in 1997.

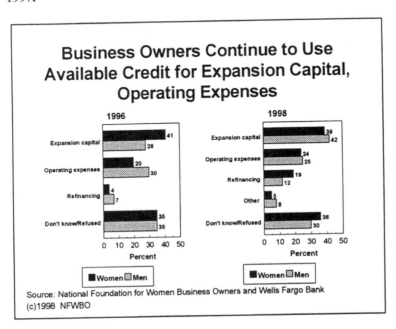

WOW! **Women business owners are forcing banks to focus more of their lending activity to women.** Yet today, most banks want access to this hot marketplace. **Wells Fargo Bank has pledged $10 billion for lending to women in business. Bank of America (Nations Bank), First Union Bank and others** are earmarking billions of dollars of credit for women business owners. Bank Boston, BankOne are exemplary regional banks offering innovative support for women.

62

WOW! **Limited bank experience in dealing with service businesses has been a major complaint about banks by women small business owners.** Although not as well as they should, banks are moving to provide services for small business owners and are giving more attention to women entrepreneurs, in that they are the fastest growth area for business today.

WOW! **Women entrepreneurs' capital resources are growing.** Among these are a number of Web sites to help entrepreneurs locate sources for funding their businesses. Some **examples are:**

- The Small Business Administration (SBA): www.sba.gov
- ACE-Net: http://ace-net.sr.unh.edu
- Capital Quest: www.usbusiness.com/capquest/home.html
- America's Business Funding Directory: www.businessfinance.com
- Venture Information Network for Entrepreneurs: www.thevin.com
- Commercial Finance Associations: www.cfr.com
  [At this site you will be asked to enter the amount and type of capital being sought. You will receive contact information and names of commercial finance companies that match your request profile.]

FINANCING HELP FOR WOMEN ENTRPRENEURS

WOW! **The Small Business Administration – Helping Women in Business Get Financing.**

- The **SBA 7(a) Program guarantees up to 90%** of loans (under $375,000) made by private financial institutions to small businesses. These loans can extend the life of the loan from 10 to 25 years and, according to *Working Woman Magazine,* were instrumental in making $1.67 billion available to women just last year.

63

- Some 45% of all micro-loans (up to $25,000) made by the SBA since 1992 have been made to women.

- Following are two examples of women venture capitalists supported by SBA and private investors. Expect more than $60 million to enter the market from these three.

- DC Women's Growth Capital Fund by Patty Abramson.

- TN Capital Access America by Whitney Johns.

WOW! Miracle Money – Venture Capital

Some venture capital groups have reached out to women and minority entrepreneurs among others. These "Angel Groups" are highly private and function mainly through networking. Here are five examples:

- A Gathering of Angels: **Santa Fe, New Mexico. Contact Tarby Bryant (505) 982-3050; anasazicap@aol.com.**

- Band of Angels: **3130 Alpine Road, Suite 200-7004, Portola Valley, CA 94028. (For business in Northern California.)**

- Investor's Circle: **San Francisco. (415) 929-4900; icmc@icircle.com.**

- Private Investor's Network: **The Michael Dingman Center for Entrepreneurship, Maryland Business School, Maryland, College Park, MD 20742; (301) 405-2144 (For mid-Atlantic area entrepreneurs.)**

- Angel Investors Program: **The New York New Media Association, (212) 785-7898; angels@nynma.org; www.nynma.org. (For new media companies.)**

64

WOW! For women business owners there has never been a better time for contracts both in the government and private sector.

WOW! Corporations are paying close attention to their relationships with women business owners. Now most are measuring both the dollars and the percentages of contracts given not only to minorities but also to women business owners.

WOW! As of 1996, every federal agency must strive to allot 5% of its business contracts to women-owned companies, thanks to an amendment by Senator Kay Bailey Hutchison (R-TX) and former Senator Carol Moseley-Braun (D-IL).

WOW! In 1996, only 1.7% of federal contract money went to women-owned firms. In 1998 the number was up to 2.2%. It was only 1.1% in 1994.

WOW! The U.S. Department of Transportation has reached its goal of 5% and the Federal Railroad Administration has surpassed that goal by awarding 7.5% of all their contracts to women-owned firms in 1997-1998.

WOW! Corporations are reporting goals and performance for the first time. Example: **Bell Atlantic will award more than $1 billion in contracts to women and minority-owned firms by December 2000.**

65

FACTS

THE CERTIFICATION PROCESS

WOW! **Certification provides official validation that a business is women-owned.** Companies and the government need to verify that a business is actually woman owned (51% to 100%), in order to receive the benefits of contracting with women suppliers. Therefore, both the private sector and the government have set up systems of certification.

WOW! Certification for the private sector is led by the **Women's Business Enterprise National Council (WBENC)** and the **National Women Business Owners Corporation (NWBOC).**

- **WBENC is a coalition of corporations, regionally focused women's business organizations and representatives of the Women's Business Enterprise community.** WBENC enhances contracting opportunities for women business enterprises (WBE's) through programs and services that are available throughout the U.S. Corporate members of WBENC have access to an internet database-WBENCLink- of enterprises that have participated in a rigorous and standardized certification process. Contact: Executive Director Susan Phillips Bari, 1155 15th Street NW, Washington, DC, 20005, (202) 862-4810, or at www.womenconnect.com/wbenc.

- **NWBOC is a national 501(c)(3) not-for-profit corporation.** NWBOC is a **sister organization to the National Association of Women Business Owners (NAWBO) and the National Foundation for Women Business Owners (NFWBO).** Contact: NWBOC, 1100 Wayne Ave., #830, Silver Spring, MD 20910, (561) 848-5066 or fax (561) 881-7364, or at http://www.wboc.org.

66

WOW! Certification for the government is done less formally, but there are several systems, including the PASS system and others. The SBA has a cooperative certification effort (Pro-Net) among the following SBA offices:

- Government Contracting;
- Minority Enterprise Development;
- Advocacy;
- Women's Business Ownership;
- Field Operations, Marketing and Customer Service;
- Chief Information Officer; and
- The National Women's Business Council.

Many government buyers shop on Pro-Net in the following way. An agency official in Idaho who wants to buy, for example, $50,000 worth of navy blue wastebaskets plugs in an SIC code and searches for companies that can fill the order. Since the listings indicate whether a business is owned by a woman or is a certified SDB, officials who need to fulfill goals for purchasing from such companies can search using those criteria. Call (800) 8ASK-SBA.

WOW! Companies are beginning to report procurement goals as never before. Leaders include J.C. Penney, Wal-Mart, Sears, AT&T, Bell Atlantic and hundreds of others.

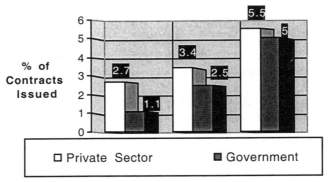

Contracts to Women-Owned Businesses

 AVON'S 10 STEPS TO STARTING A BUSINESS

- **Believe in Yourself.** Maintaining a positive attitude and believing that you can make your entrepreneurial dreams come true – these are the keys to future successes.

- **Define Your Goals.** Before your jump in, know where you are heading. Time spent developing both short- and long-term goals is perhaps the most important time you will ever spend on your business.

- **Contemplate Being on Your Own.** The independent business lifestyle isn't for everyone. Consider how well you like working alone, managing your own time, and performing a multitude of tasks – often without any support staff.

- **Choose the Best Business for You.** You are far more likely to succeed if you choose a business or product that really excites you. Next, it is important to determine if there is a market for what you are going to promote and sell. Tackle something with low start-up costs, but with potential for real growth.

- **Consider the Options.** Some entrepreneurs prefer to purchase existing businesses. Others buy franchises. Increasing numbers of women today are choosing to work as independent contractors, receiving support from a large company without taking major financial risks.

- **Write Your Business Plan**. Before you get your business cards printed, you must have a solid blueprint for business growth. Defining your product, potential customers and competition will underscore the risks and rewards that lie ahead.

- **Ask the Experts.** The type of business you choose will determine the level of professional advice you will need. If you are starting a small home-based business, a chat with you accountant about tax implications may be enough. You may also need to speak with an attorney and banker if you are planning a larger venture.

- **Arrange Financing.** Make sure you will have access to a line of credit or the funds you need before you begin. The key reason many businesses fail is under-capitalization.

- **Organize. Organize. Organize**. After you've opened your business, you're likely to be too busy to handle details, so make sure that you have taken care of child care needs and have organized your workspace in advance.

- **Network Your Way to Success.** Join professional organizations. Attend classes and seminars. Meet as many people as you can who might become potential customers or help you build your business in other ways.

WOW! 10 REASONS FOR BUSINESS SUCCESS

- Your **product or service** is well suited to the market.
- You've completed a **business plan** before beginning your operation.
- You've completed a **market analysis**.
- You are keeping accurate **financial controls**, are frugal and squeeze every penny until it screams.
- You have a high degree of **competence, ability and integrity**.
- Your time **management, administration policies and objectives** are real and results-oriented.
- You have **determination, patience and persistence**.
- Your good at **communicating among staff** and have an open door policy.
- There is a **strong momentum in sales**, and everyone is market driven.
- There is **concern for the customer** all the time.

WOW! 10 REASONS FOR BUSINESS FAILURE

- There is a **lack of direction**, and employees are reactive, not proactive.
- You are **impatient**, wanting too much too soon.
- **Greed is a motivator**.
- You are **impetuous and act without thinking or listening to gut feelings**.
- There are **poor cost controls**, no **budgeting** and overspending.
- **Product quality is poor**.
- There is **insufficient working capital**.
- You **fail to anticipate market trends**.
- **Indecisiveness and the inability to make a decision** holds you back.
- **A lack of managerial experience** and rejection of advisors.

[Source: "What Every Entrepreneur Needs To Know," The Entrepreneurial Center]

FACTS

BUSINESS PLANS

A carefully constructed business plan is an essential tool to map out a course of action and a necessary document when looking for financing. Many entrepreneurs say that the process of writing the plan is a valuable educational exercise. There are many ways to organize a business plan and many books and software programs to help you through the process. <u>A good plan needs to cover the following six areas:</u>

1) Executive Summary: A description of the business that is so well thought out that the reader wants to read the rest of the plan. The summary pages should be able to stand on their own and include who the customer is, how much money is necessary to run the business, goals, strategy and key competitive factors.

2) Business Description: Give background information, a history of the company and short- and long-term objectives.

3) Market Analysis and Marketing Strategy: An industry overview and market outlook that highlights key opportunities should be included, as should research and analysis on the market, including your competition. Measuring the market size and listing trends are helpful. Develop a full marketing plan, including strategy, and information on sales and distribution, pricing, advertising, and promotion.

4) Business Organization: Include the company's legal structure, key personnel, staffing, facilities, equipment, research, design, manufacturing and development work you will do.

5) Financial Information: Give the best estimates possible, as well as a balance sheet, income statement and cash-flow statement

71

covering a three-year period. Identify sources of financing and when you expect to break even.

6) Appendix: Additional helpful information, such as resumes of management, documents, drawings and other supporting materials, should be included.
[Source: Take Control of Your Life: Start Your Own Business, Ten Practical Steps To Get You Started, Avon Products, Inc.]

GLOBAL WOMEN ENTREPRENEURS

WOW! If you've never heard of Women's World Banking (WWB) it's probably because most of the 200,000 loans they make each year, averaging $300 each, go to over 500,000 clients in developing countries.

WWB seeks to expand the economic participation of millions of poor women entrepreneurs through direct services and influencing government, bank and business policies and practices. "There's something so powerful about...the simple idea of women and credit, and credit as the link to business development," said WWB's president

RESOURCES FOR WOMEN ENTREPRENEURS

 BOOKS – Examples:

How to Prepare and Present a Business Plan; By Joseph R. Mancuso; Paperback – Prentice Hall, $15.00.

Anatomy of a Business Plan: A Step-by-Step guide to Starting Smart, Building the Business and Securing Your Company's Future (3rd Edition); By Linda Pinson and Jerry A. Jinnett;   Paperback – 224 pages (March

1996) $19.95. Award winning bestseller. This step-by-step guide helps entrepreneurs create effective, results-oriented business plans.

The Service Business Planning Guide: The Complete Hand-book for Creating a Winning Business Plan for Any Service Company; By Warren G. Purdy and Bradford W. Ketchum; Paperback – 336 pages (October 1996) $19.95. Focuses on developing industry-specific business plans from professional services to contractors to food services and beyond. Written for the entrepreneur, small business owners and managers, this guide provides techniques and resources and offers do-it-yourself worksheets and advice on using the Internet and electronic commerce as marketing tools.

The Perfect Business Plan Made Simple; By William Lasher, Ph.D.; Paperback – 278 pages (March 1994) $12.95. Readers are shown how to write and sell a quality business plan. This guide covers the business-planning process and has appendices of business plans for different types of businesses.

The Complete Book of Business Plans: Simple Steps to Writing a Powerful Business Plan; (Small Business Sourcebooks); By Joseph A. Covello and Brian J. Hazelgren; Paperback – 320 pages (April 1994) $19.95.

The Women's New Selling Game; By Carole Hyatt; $14.95. Hyatt offers advice on how to increase financial rewards through greater responsibility and more precise skills.

Business Capital for Women: An Essential Handbook for Entrepreneurs; By Emily Card and Adam Miller; $16.95.

Money Smart Secrets for the Self-Employed; By Linda Stern; $20. Stern presents ways to cut small business expenses.

Minding Her Own Business: The Self-Employed Women's Guide to

73

Taxes and Record Keeping; By Jan Zobel; $16.95.

Mompreneurs: A Mother's Practical Step-by-Step Guide To Work-at-Home; By Ellen H. Parlapiano and Patricia Cobe; $13. Offers means by which to establish a home business without letting professional enterprises interfere with family life.

About My Sister's Business: The Black Woman's Road Map to Successful Entrepreneurship; By Fran Harris; $12.   Harris offers advice on the starting and maintaining of businesses.

The Women's Business Resource Guide; By Barbara Litman; $18.95. A comprehensive resource guide for the aspiring female business-owner.

Hers: The Wise Woman's Guide to Starting a Business on $2,000 or Less; By Carol Milano; $16.95. Offers advice and resources for those who want to start a business on a limited budget.

Sister CEO; By Cheryl Broussard; $21.95. A comprehensive guide to entrepreneurship.

1998-99 Business Women's Network Directory; Published annually by the Business Women's Network; $100. Provides over 2,300 profiles of women's business organizations (1450) and Web sites (850) throughout the United States and Canada.

WOW. MAGAZINES AND PAMPHLETS – Examples:

Starting a Business, by the Small Business Administration. Questions to ask about yourself and your business plans before you get started. Discusses financing and explains the four types of business ownership, 10 pages (1996 SBA 589E.) Free.

Resource Directory for Small Business Management. Lists publications and videotapes useful for starting and managing a successful small business. 5 pages. (1996, SBA 362E.) $0.50.

Running a Small Business, by the Small Business Administration. Discusses sales and marketing; record keeping; finding advisors; partners; personnel; patents/trademarks/copyrights, and financial concerns. 11 pages. (1996, SBA 597D.) Free.

Selling a Business, by the Small Business Administration. How to find a buyer, work with a broker, assess what your business is worth, handle your customer list, and finance the sale. 12 pages. (1996, SBA 598D.) Free.

Americans with Disabilities Act: Guide for Small Businesses, by the U. S. Department of Justice. Discusses basic requirements businesses must follow to ensure that facilities are accessible. Includes toll-free sources for more assistance. 15 pages. (1996, DOJ 586E.) Free.

SBA Programs & Services, by the Small Business Administration, Discusses how SBA can help you start or expand a business. Lists phone numbers, online information, business counseling and training, lending programs and much more. 23 pages. (1996, SBA 588E.) Free.

Today's Black Woman Newsletter
Contact: Jennifer Keitt, 888-TBWOMAN. The newsletter offers helpful information on entrepreneurship, financial planning, and other issues relevant to the working woman.

75

WEB SITES – Examples:

First Steps: How to Start a Small Business
www.sba.gov – The SBA web site for starting a new business provides complete data and advice. Q & As to research, writing your business plan, financing, planning and researching your new business.

Business Start-Ups Online
www.entrepreneurmag.com/bizstarts.hts – From *Entrepreneur Magazine* . Presents entrepreneurial ideas, advice columns, and Q&A's to help you make informed decisions.

Entrepreneur Magazine
www.entrepreneurmag.com

Entrepreneur Radio Network
www.//ern.amradio.net

Ecommerce Weekly
www.eweekly .com

International Entrepreneur Association.
www.theiea.com

Write Your Business Plan
www.womenswire.com – Members of Women's Wire can access this step by step interactive outline for writing a business plan.

Business Start
www.wp.com/fredfish – A resource site for entrepreneurs.

Free Business Reports

www.webcom.com/seaquest/sbrc/reports – From "Finding and Starting a Business" to "Running your Business more Effectively," you can download reports to help you in your new business start-up, and manage your business effectively and efficiently.

Internet Business Start-Ups

www.actium1.com – Information online business planning, online business opportunities and online business resources.

The Small Business Administration Business Plan Guide

www.sba.gov – The SBA provides online comprehensive direction in writing a business plan with guidance in seeking loans from financial institutions, private investors and the SBA.

The NationsBank Small Business Center

www.nationsbank.com – This web site provides assistance for those looking to start or expand a business.

Small Business Advisor Site

isquare.com – This site offers a newsletter and a comprehensive resource list.

Franchise Information

franchise1.com – This site offers a franchise company directory as well as information on articles and trade shows.

HOME OFFICE - HOME BUSINESS

WOW! 60% of all women-owned businesses started as home office operations.

WOW! Of the 9,000,000 women-owned businesses in the US, 80% or 7,200,000 are either small office or home office firms. Of these, 45%, or 4,050,000, are home office operations.

WOW! **Most Successful Home Office Businesses for Women:**

1. Consulting and Services
2. Computer Services and Programming
3. Financial Consulting and Services
4. Marketing and Advertising
5. Medical Practices and Services
6. Graphics and Visual Arts
7. Public Relations
8. Real Estate
9. Writing
10. Independent Sales.

WOW! By the year 2002, one in every five households in the U.S. will have at least one adult working full-time from home.

WOW! By the year 2000, 20% of all travel agents will be home-based.

WOW! **70% of businesses fail within the first three years,** with the primary cause being the lack of adequate funding. However, home-based businesses have higher success rates because of limited overhead expense.

WOW! **Owners of full-time, home-based businesses have incomes that are 20% higher than the income of the average household,** according to the New York research firm IDC/Link. They also report that almost 11% of households that included a home-based business had an income last year of more than $100,000.

WOW! **The top 10 states for small office/home office businesses** in 1998 are: (1) California, (2) Texas, (3) New York, (4) Illinois, (5) Florida, (6) Pennsylvania, (7) Michigan, (8) Washington, (9) Minnesota, and (10) Ohio.

RESOURCES FOR HOME-BASED BUSINESSES

WOW! **Associations – Examples:**

- **The National Association of the Self-Employed** (NASE); (262) 462-2100. www.nase.org
- **The Home Office Association of America** (HOAA) (212) 980-4622.
- **National Associaton of Home-Based Businesses** (NAHBB) (800) 479-9710. www.nahbb/index.shtml
- **American Home Business Association** (AHBA) (800) 758-8500. www.homebusiness.com

79

FACTS

WOW! Internet Resources - Examples:

- **Work-At-Home Moms**: www.wahm.com
- **Home-Based Working Moms**: www.hbwn.com
- **Bizymoms**: www.bizymom.com; www.snowcrest.net/folger
- **Working Mom Home Business Resources**: www.members.tripod.com/~workinmoms
- **Formerly Employed Mothers at the Leading Edge**: www.femalehome.org
- **CyberMom**: www.thecybermom.com
- **Moms Network Exchange**: www.momsnetwork.com
- www.everydaybiz.hypermart.net/women

WOW! Books and Guides - Examples:

- *The Joy of Working from Home* by Jeff Berner (1994) $12.95.
- *Launching Your Home-Based Business* by David Bangs, Jr. and Andi Axman (1997) $22.95.
- *Marketing for the Home-Based Business* by Jeffrey Davidson (1993) $13.95.
- *How to Start a Successful Home Business* by Karen Cheney & Lesley Alderman (1997) $10.99.
- *How to Raise a Family and a Career Under One Roof* by Lisa Roberts (1997) $15.95.
- *How to Run Your Own Home Business* by Caralee Smith Kern & Tammara Hoffman Wolfgram (1994) $9.95.
- *Home Business Made Easy* by David Hanania (1998) $19.95.
- *The Home Office & Small Business Answer Book* by Janet Attard (1993) $19.95.

80

CHAPTER 4: FINANCE

W0W! **Women have capital and assets: Nearly 1 million American women have annual incomes exceeding $100,000.**

W0W! More than 50% of US households with high net worth are now headed by women. **Some 40% of households with assets of more than $600,000 or more are headed by women.**

W0W! **Women are focusing on finance:** In her book, <u>When Are You Entitled to New Underwear and Other Major Financial Decisions,</u> Eileen Michaels of Legg Mason discusses how important it is for women to plan for financial independence. The Beardstown Ladies argue that women must take financial responsibility for themselves.

WOMEN ARE INVESTING

W0W! From Prudential Securities: March, 1999:
80% of women are open to new investment strategies. Prudential Securities did a benchmark study comparing men and women investors in 1995, and they updated it in March, 1999.   They provide comprehensive data including the following:

- In 1995, 72% of women said they were open to considering new investment opportunities and strategies; in 1998 some 80% of women had this view;

- In 1995, 41% of women said they often put off making financial decisions for fear of making a mistake. In 1998 that number had dropped to 32%;

- 11% of women have more confidence in financial terminology than in the past, but there is still a high expression of confusion. In 1995, 69% of women said financial terminology was confusing; in 1998 the number had dropped to 58%.

- **Women's investing confidence has grown**; they are less fearful of making mistakes with money, and they are more willing to consider taking risks on investments than they were in 1995. **In 1998 only 25% of women considered investing risky**, a decrease from 45% in 1995.

- **More women in 1998 (38% vs. the 1995 figure of 26%) said they are willing to take substantial risks in hopes of making substantial gains.**

- However, the study found **that men still outnumber women as the most active and assertive investors.**

- **Both men and women have become more confident in their abilities to invest.**

Investors of both sexes are:

- **optimistic about the future,** (women 73%, men, 76%);
- **look forward to retirement** (men 71%, women 72 percent);
- **have a specific savings plan for retirement** (men, 77%, women 69%);
- are **active investors** (women, 69%, men 71%).

- The study found that men still do most of the investing for families. Only 15% of married women describe themselves as the main decision maker regarding investments. However, 78% said they share the decision-making responsibility.

- Among married men, about one-third say they are the main decision maker and two-thirds say they share the responsibility.

WOW! Women are 47% of stock owners, according to a 1997 survey done by Peter Hart and Associates for NASDAQ.

WOW! 35% of all first-time buyers of financial products are women.

WOW! Women make the investment decisions in 32% of households where investments are made. **Women are a critical part of investment decision-making in another 51% of all households.**

WOW! Women investing for their families **say their primary investment vehicle is the 401(k) plan.**

WOW! Investment seminars aimed at women are increasing exponentially, as are books, magazines, television shows, and web sites targeted at the women investor.

WOW! Investment books for women are prominent in bookstores and on the web: There were no new women's investment books in 1985, and only four in 1992. However, in 1998 more than 20 were published.

83

WOW! **There has also been a proliferation of books and booklets aimed at women by investment firms; 90% of the major investment firms are producing such materials.** Example: Oppenheimer & Company produced *A Woman's Guide to Investing* which portrays the difference in investing styles of men and women.

WOW! **Magazines** are covering women and investing. *Fortune,* in the March 29, 1999 issue, ran an article called "Women really could use special advice about investing." *Worth Magazine* printed a women's investing supplement called *Equity.*

WOW! **Women financial planners are proliferating.** This trend is helpful because women are generally more comfortable with advice from respected women in the field of finance. Oppenheimer & Company funded a survey which reported that "women felt alienated by financial advisers." Alexandra Armstrong, a leading financial planner in Washington, D.C., was one of the first women leaders of the Institute for Financial Planners.

WOW! **Investment firms are all developing their women's programs.** For example,

- **Oppenheimer & Co.**, which was the first company to focus on women, has an array of investment products and seminars for women.

- **Merrill Lynch** has long had major women's programs. Merrill produces *A Woman's Guide to Wealth and Management* and *You and Your Money.*

- **Salomon Smith Barney** sponsors seminars and publishes materials for women investors like their brochure on financial advice called *Women in Transition.*

- **Edward Jones** is sponsoring women's programs nationwide, working with the Small Business Administration, the American Business Women's Association and others.

- **Citibank and Chase** have long held seminars for women. Both have specific marketing materials such as Money Matters for Women, in which one of Citibanks's financial planning experts focuses on savings.

WOW! **Accounting firms are developing women's programs and materials .** Among the best known is the package of materials from Ernst & Young, entitled *Financial Planning for Women.*

WOW! **5% of female decision-makers are willing to take substantial risk for the chance to gain substantial return ,compared to 11% of men.**[3]

WOW! **Women need to save more and invest more** given their longevity. Women live an average of six years longer than men.

WOW! Virtually all studies demonstrate that women are more conservative in investing than men. Example: In a study by Long Island University's Center for Women's Studies, 7% of women owned CDs in their retirement plans vs. 52% of men.

---

[3] Investment Company Institute Study in 1995.

WOW! Women's Investment clubs have been established in virtually every community in the U.S. It is reported that women's clubs beat the returns of male-only investment clubs at return rates of 17.3% vs. 15.6%, respectively.

WOW! In 1997, there were 16,000 all-female investment clubs, and the number continues to increase by 35% a decade. 66% of the investment clubs consist of women.

WOW! With the increasing number of women investing, women will create more wealth in future. There will be a 40% increase by the year 2010. The chart following illustrates this increase.

U.S .Private Wealth			
Total		Women's Share	
$Trillion		Trillion	Percent
1995	$14 Tr	$2.2 Tr	16%
2010	$25 Tr	$12.5Tr	56%
Change	+11 Tr	+10 Tr	176%

WOW! The financial confidence gap between men and women is narrowing. Men's confidence has not changed: 29% feel "quite competent," according to studies in 1994 and 1999. Women's confidence, however, has risen over the same period: from 16% in 1994, to 22% in 1999.

WOW! Paine Webber has profiled women investors and provides the following information about them:

86

- More than one third of women in the US are investors.

- A **majority of women investors say that 10% is the minimum annual rate of return** required before they consider their investments to be "good.

- **Women are more likely to compare their investments with last year's performance of their investments,** while men are more likely to compare them with the Dow Jones Industrial Average.

- **54% of women, compared with 33% of men, feel they do not understand finance**.

- **Women investors want to retire at 59.7 years old, on average**.

WOW! **Women entrepreneurs are twice as likely as their male counterparts to begin investing this year (1999),** according to The National Foundation For Women Business Owners.

WOW! **The National Association of Investors Corporation h a s 700,000 members, and some 65,370 of those members, almost 10%, are women. The investment world is waking up to women.**

WOW! According to a **University of California at Davis study, Wall Street women are better investors than men.**

WOW! **Women are more cautious investors but as they gain knowledge and experience they tend to be more aggressive**.

87

WOW! Women tend to want financial advice, while men prefer to manage their own investments.

WOW! Women tend to buy and hold investments. 44% of women investors track the performance of their stocks and mutual funds at least once a week.

WOW! 64% of men gave themselves a grade of "A" or "B" on investment knowledge or expertise, compared to 54% of women.

WOW! Women were less likely to know the Dow Jones average: 89% of men vs. 56% of women were familiar with it.

WOW! Women are trying to learn more about financial investing. 36% said they had read a book or article about investing in the last month, as compared to 46% of men.

WOW! Women who are normally open, sharing and consummate networkers, **reported they are less likely to discuss investments than men**: 47% of women vs. 56% of men.

WOW! Women, despite the millions of dollars now being expended to reach women investors, **lack the information needed to manage their finances**. A 1998 Study by Brandeis University National Center for Women and Aging as reported in Ernst & Young's <u>Financial Planning for Women</u> provided the following data:

- 50% of those who had not consulted a financial professional said they did not know how to select one.

- 46% of the women surveyed worried about trusting advisors.

- 39% of the women surveyed did not know whether their consultant was certified or registered by an accrediting organization.

- 50% were uncertain about steps to take if they were to face a serious problem with a financial advisor.

WOW! Salomon Smith Barney is an investment firm that affirms the importance of women's investments. **The firm claims that its client base has increased to more than 40% female in 1997-1998.**

WOW! The market for women investors is so hot that most of the firms cite enhanced efforts to recruit women brokers. Salomon Smith Barney, Legg Mason, Merrill Lynch, Paine Webber, Morgan Stanley Dean Witter, and others tell BWN of **significant increases in women's recruitment and women's investment.**

WOW! Women investors have been profiled in the Bankers Trust Corporation "Women on Wall Street" study which was conducted by Yankelovich Partners in New York City. The study revealed the following about women investors:

- 46% listed retirement as their top investment goal, and 89% listed retirement as one of their top three goals;

- 40% gave themselves a "C" or higher as investors;

89

- 53% felt that men have more time to spend on investing;

- 68% thought that women take fewer investment risks than do men;

- 48% believe that investment firms market differently to men than to women;

- 59% have their investable assets in stocks;

- 20% have a written financial plan.

WOW! 46% of stock owners have graduated from college.

WOW! 23% of stock owners have some college education but did not receive a degree, and another 12% attended a two-year college or received vocational training after high school.

WOW! 23% of stock owners had no educational experience past high school and 2% did not complete high school.

WOW! 66% of women (75% men) allocate some of their income to savings or investments.

WOW! The median figure for household savings for women was **$7,300 in 1997** compared to **$15,400 for men.**

90

© Business Women's Network, Washington, DC 20036
(800) 48-WOMEN
http://www.bwni.com

FACTS

INVESTOR RESOURCES EXAMPLES

WOW! Web sites:

- **Armchair Millionaire:** Get rich slowly but surely in five easy steps for women investors. www.armchairmillionaire.com

- **Beatrice's Web Guide:** Shortcut to useful sites and offers content specifically designed for women. www.bguide.com

- **Buck Starts Here:** Nancy Dunnan financial advisor. www.talks.com/bucks

- **Money Mode (Women's Wire):** www.womenswire.com/money

- **The Women's Network:** www.ivillage.com

WOW! Resources in Print:

- Ernst & Young's Financial Planning for Women. John Wiley & Sons

- The 10 Minute Guide to Retirement for Women. Hannon; MacMillan

- Savvy Investing for Women: Strategies for a Self Made Wall Street Millionaire. Jupiter; Prentice Hall

91

CHAPTER 5: CORPORATE WORLD & WOMEN

WOMEN HOLDING TOP POSITIONS

WOW! The number of women who rank among the top five wage earners within Fortune 500 company has doubled since 1995. Now 2.7% of the 2,320 top earners, or 63, are women. However, 24% of companies still have no women corporate officers.

WOW! Women hold 49% of all managerial and professional positions. **By the year 2010, it is projected that women will hold 50% of top management jobs.**

(Source: Catalyst Census of Women Corporate Officers and Top Earners, Catalyst 1998)

WOW! **The median compensation for the top 5 female CEO's for 1996 was $981,192.** Note: that this was less than the $1.9 million median for Fortune 500 male CEO's.

WOW! **Companies value being named to a list that identifies them as a "Best Company for Working Women." It is a powerful recruitment and marketing tool.** The *Bureau of National Affairs*, in its October 26, 1998 issue, states that such ranking by magazines have created a coveted honor. Companies seek to be on the lists of such publications as *Working Woman*, *Working Mother*, *Forbes* and *Fortune* magazines.

For Example:
- **First Tennessee Bank** values its rating and has done a bottom-line evaluation of its results. It says, "the applicant flow at the Memphis-based bank is very strong. As a result, we can fill jobs 50% faster than the industry average."
- **The Calvert Group** reports that it has hired applicants who targeted Calvert as an employer because of the culture, work ethics and benefits package. Data shows that turnover was cut 100% over a five-year period from 1986 to 1991.
- **KPMG, Hewlett-Packard, Southwest Airlines, Deloitte and Touche** and others cite their high rates as a way to help get the message out to the employees and the American public that they are good employers for women.

WOW! A 1995 Federal Glass Ceiling Commission Report found that women held only 3%-5% of the senior-level jobs in major corporations.

WOW! Top 10 companies based on percentage of women in their work force:

1. Kelly Services	80%
2. CIGNA	74%
3. AETNA	73%
4. Nordstrom	72%
5. GAP	71.6%
6. AVON	70%
7. Lincoln National	70%
8. Home Savings of America	69.8%
9. Dayton Hudson	69%
10. Sallie Mae	68.6%

WOW! Companies with highest percent of women at the VP level and above:

1. American Express	67%
2. Lincoln National	60%
3. Pitney Bowes	58%
4. Fannie Mae	56%
5. Scholastic	45.4%
6. GAP	39.9%
7. Nordstrom	38.8%
8. Kelly Services	38.7%
9. Sallie Mae	35.9%
10. Home Savings of America	32%

[Source: Working Woman Magazine, September 1998]

95

WOW! Companies with the highest percentage of women managers:

•	GAP	81%
•	Kelly Services	78%
•	Nordstrom	71%
•	Scholastic	61%
•	AETNA	60%

[Source: Working Woman Magazine, September 1998]

WOW! **The 1998 Catalyst Census of Women Corporate Officers and Top Earners, looked at the Fortune 500 companies** and provided the following pertinent data:

- **Thirty-three companies (6.6%) have women filling 25% or more of corporate officer positions.** Companies at the top of that list include H.F. Ahmanson (50% before absorption into larger enterprise), Nordstrom (40%), CoreStates Financial (40% before absorption), Fannie Mae and Pacific Health Systems (39%).
- In 1998, for the first time, **more than half of the Fortune 500 companies (259 companies) had more than one woman corporate officer**. This was an increase of 11% over the 1997 figures.
- **The number of companies with no women corporate officers also increased, to 123.**
- **Women held only two CEO positions in 1998,** Jill Barad of Mattel and Marion Sandler at Golden West Financial. Of the **7 most powerful positions,** women held only 3.8%.
- **Catalyst projects women will fill 13% of corporate officer positions in the year 2000, and 17% by the year 2005.**

WOW! The chart below illustrates salary levels of men and women in the Fortune 500 earners:

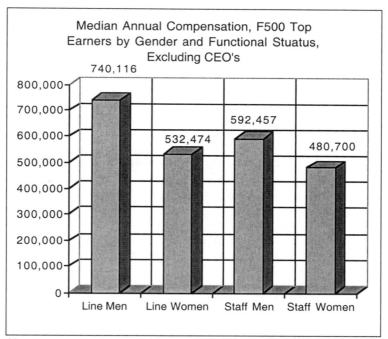

Median Annual Compensation, F500 Top Earners by Gender and Functional Stuatus, Excluding CEO's

[Source: Catalyst Census of Women Corporate Officers and Top Earners, Catalyst 1998]

97

WOW! FACTS

CORPORATE LEADERSHIP EXAMPLES

Johnson & Johnson:
Of the Johnson & Johnson workforce, 49.9% women (15.9% are VP's and higher, 34% are managers). Women's Leadership Initiative networking relationships. Mentoring – Executive women mentor up across 180 J& J divisions; mentoring program accelerates advancement of women through middle management.

Xerox:
Of the Xerox workforce, 33% women (11.4% VP's and above, 28% mangers) Women and Technology Center encourages women to pursue careers in technology; Women's Alliance and other coalitions.

IBM Corporation:
In the last three years, the number of women executives at IBM worldwide has nearly doubled. Even more impressively, the company has accomplished this feat across cultural lines: Two years ago, there were nine female executives in European operations; today there are 22. Louis Gerstner, IBM CEO, created the IBM Women's Task Force "to facilitate the recognition and development of women at IBM." One result has been the Global Women's Leadership Forum, encouraging cross-cultural exchange among IBM women executives.

Home Savings America:
With 409 branches in California, Texas, and Florida, in addition to a stock brokerage, and an insurance brokerage, Home Savings is one of the country's biggest consumer banks. It has plans for further growth through acquisition, and intends to grow the number of women executives. More than ten managers, three of them women, have gone through Rinehart's executive assistant program, in which they work with the CEO and other company officers to sharpen their strengths.

98

WOW!
FACTS

Cigna:

Last year, 40% of Cigna's management promotions went to women. The insurer offers an enviable array of work-life programs, from takeout dinners to Great Escapes, a childcare program that fills in the gaps during school holidays. Cigna concerns itself with the needs of manager-moms in other ways as well. The recently created part-time manager track already has 600 participants, including 38 women at levels ranging form assistant vice president to senior vice president. In addition, 387 executive women work part-time.

Hannaford Brothers Company:

Hannaford operates 146 supermarkets on the East Coast, mainly regional chains such as Shop 'n' Save and Wilson's Supermarkets. Its consistent promotion of women makes it stand out. Instead of simply promoting store managers from regional offices to headquarters, the firm circulates them through a variety of operating positions; one human resources manager, for example, just finished a stint in real estate and is moving into accounting. This way, managers get some retail experience as well as insight into the business's big picture.

Bristol-Myers Squibb Company:

Last year, Bristol's domestic sales force was 52% female. Women managers have always been a force within Bristol-Myers; however, programs to track diversity began just last year. Bristol-Myers plans to develop women managers by identifying cultural barriers to advancement, then creating programs to break them down while linking diversity initiatives to business goals.

Lincoln National Corporation:

Since launching its Women at Work Task Force in 1993, Lincoln National has helped women advance fast. Not only does the company require managers to measure their progress, but it also chooses outside vendors-especially recruiters-with track records of promoting women in management. The company supports flexible work-life arrangements.

99

WOMEN ON CORPORATE BOARDS

WOW! Catalyst in New York City conducts an annual *Catalyst Census of Women Board Directors of the Fortune 500.* **Their 1998 Census provided the following data:**

- **More Women are being placed on corporate boards than ever before – 11.1% of all corporate board seats are now held by women,** and it is projected that the number will grow to more than 12% by the year 2000.

- **Currently 86% of Fortune 500 companies,** 429 companies in all, **have women on their boards.** That number is up from 419 companies last year. One-third of them, or 188 companies, have more than one female board member.

- **The number of Fortune 500 companies with 2 or more women board members jumped from 146 in 1994 to 188 in 1998.** The chart following illustrates this data:

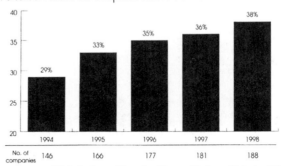

Percent of Fortune 500 Companies With Two or More Women Directors

1998 Catalyst Census of Women Board Directors of the Fortune 500, Catalyst, 1998

The 1998 Catalyst Census also collected data on the occupations of women directors as shown below:

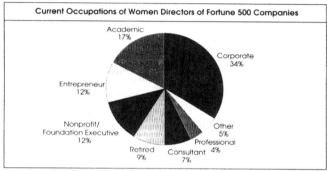

Current Occupations of Women Directors of Fortune 500 Companies

1998 Catalyst Census of Women Board Directors of the Fortune 500, Catalyst, 1998

 More than half of the top 500 industrial companies now have women directors: 260 of the top 500 manufacturing companies and 323 of the top 500 service companies.

 CEOs speak out on the importance of recruiting and advancing women. Example: Arthur Ryan, CEO of Prudential, proudly reports that in 1998 70% of promotions were to women.

 Of the total 6,064 board seats among the Fortune 500 companies, **women hold 671 or 11.1%.**

101

WOW! Catalyst projects that there will be gender parity on **Fortune 500 Boards by the year 2064,** based on the rate of change since 1993, the first year of the Catalyst Census.

- One company, Golden West Financial Corporation, had already achieved and exceeded parity with five women and four men directors.

- Several companies are approaching parity with 40% or more Directors being women-Avon Products, Inc., Golden West Financial and Gannett Co., Inc.

Leading Corporations:

Company	No. of Female Directors	Total	% Female
TIAA-CREF	9	35	25.7
Avon Products	6	13	46.2
Fannie Mae	5	18	27.8
Golden West Financial	5	9	55.6
Bell Atlantic	4	22	18.2
Aetna	4	13	30.8
Consolidated Edison	4	13	30.8
Gannett	4	10	40

WOW! The industries with the highest percent of companies having no women on boards are computer/data service, engineering and construction. **More than 40% of companies in these industries still have no women board directors.**

102

CORPORATE BOARD INITIATIVES

Examples:

Board of Directors, Inc. is a private, nonprofit corporation and professional advocacy to encourage good corporate governance practices including inclusion of women as directors. (404) 652-1818. Atlanta, GA.

Catalyst Inc. of New York runs Corporate Board Placement (CBP). Catalyst has developed a computerized database of information on more than 2,000 women, filled major assignments, and produced a comprehensive board study for the past several years. For information, contact: Corporate Board Placement (212) 514-7600.

The National Association of Corporate Directors (NACD), Washington DC, provides a comprehensive resource for men and women. Its focus is primarily the mid-level companies. For information, call (202) 775-0509.

Boardroom Bound seeks to increase women and minority board participation as well as educate companies on advantages of board diversification. Call (202) 296-9237 for additional information. Linda Bollinger, founder and CEO, is aggressive in the training for women and minorities on boards.

The International Alliance and its Director's Resource Program, with Two able co-chairs, is working to provide programming, a resource service and help to its networks. Call (410) 472-4221.

The Boston Club began its efforts by publishing a book presenting leading women candidates for corporate boards. Then they focused on developing a database. Call (617) 965-0922.

Financial Women's Association of NY is one of the nation's most dynamic nonprofit professional organizations. It advances women in their finance careers with special events and board opportunities. Call (212) 533-2141.

National Women's Economic Alliance has worked with leading corporations for the past ten years to identify qualified people who happen to be women for corporate board positions. The Alliance holds regular "A Seat at the Table" seminars, which educate women on the board selection and recruitment process. Call (202) 393-5257.

Women Chamber Of Commerce Of Texas, with its 550 members, serves as an advocate in the legislature and encourages more women to serve on boards and commissions. The Chamber is primarily concerned with economic parity for women, women in leadership roles and participating in policy-making that affects women economically. Call (512) 476-4140.

Rochester Women's Network (RWN) efforts have been extensive. RWN sought and captured 35 leading women candidates for the database. Then they set a goal to double that number to 70. RWN targeted 25 companies and produced a report revealing that in 1985 there were only seven women on corporate boards in the Rochester area; now there are over 156. The movement has witnessed a change of approach from database development to advocacy. Call (716) 271-4182; http://www.rwn.org

Executive Women of New Jersey provides an executive search service for corporations to help them find female directors and increase the number of women on corporate boards. Call (732) 530-4098

Committee of 200 reports more on corporate boards, many of whom are listed in their monthly newsletter. One of the objectives of the Committee is, "to see more women in top business management/ownership positions and corporate board positions." Call (312) 751-3477; www.c200.org.

104

FACTS

Colorado Women's Leadership Coalition aims to increase the number of women on Colorado state boards and commissions by 50%. In order to develop programs to reach its goal, the Coalition has conducted research on leadership opportunities. The goal is developing an effective program for placing qualified women on for-profit boards of businesses and corporations. Call (303) 221-74334 or www.gossamer-moon.com/cwlc.

WOW! Why Do Women Want To Serve On Boards?
It can be difficult to shatter the glass ceiling and getting on a board of directors is another way to affect change at the highest levels of management. To affect lasting change. BWN projects women on corporate boards to be

- **15% by 2005**
- **20% by 2010**
- **25% by 2015.**

BWN projects women of color on boards to increase to nearly 100%; from 58% by 2005.

WORK-LIFE

WOW! The quality of worker's jobs and the supportiveness of their workplaces are the most powerful predictors of productivity, job satisfaction, commitment to employers, and retention.

WOW! In a recent survey of dual-career marriages by Catalyst, the benefits that respondents said they most wanted companies to offer were:

- Flexible hours   85%
- Cafeteria-style benefits   79%
- Family leave   74%
- Customized career path   69%
- Home office telecommuting   65%

105

Facts

▪	Formal flexible work program	63%
▪	Company supported childcare	53%
▪	Spouse relocation assistance	46%
▪	Eldercare support	38%

WOW! A Workforce Management Study of over 10,000 workers in 13 industrialized companies determined that **employers are not meeting employee's core needs**.

WOW! Studies have shown that **flexible schedules** offer a **tool for managing both costs and productivity. Part time employment, compressed work schedules** and **telecommuting** proved the most popular approaches to flex-time.

WOW! **59% of working women, versus 73% of working men are satisfied**, for the most part, **with their ability to balance work and family.**

WOW! In a survey, by Catalyst, of 802 members of dual-career couples, **70% of women said they would leave their job if not satisfied.**

WOW! Catalyst offers the following **strategies to reduce turnover among high potential women:**

- *Communicate to women that they are valued.* Communicate it often - in writing, verbally, with compensation, with development opportunities, and with high-visibility assignments.
  - *Remove hidden barriers to advancement.* Get help if you need it to design tailored strategies that address your unique issues and that fit your operations and culture.

106

© Business Women's Network, Washington, DC 20036
(800) 48-WOMEN
http://www.bwni.com

FACTS

- *Address the work/life balance issues seriously.* Check out the best practices in more flexible work arrangements and support programs.

WOW! Corporate Marketing on the Web

Some examples of Web sites marketing to women are:

- **Women on Wall Street (Bankers Trust)**: www.bankerstrust.com
- **Women's Initiative Network**: www.deloitte.com
- **Women's Health (Eli Lilly)**: www.elililly.com
- **Women on their Way (Wyndham)**: www.womenbusinesstravelers.com
- **Women's Link (Bristol Myers** site): www.memberslink.com
- **Executive Women's Web site (Delta Airlines):** www.delta.com

WOW! Increased Working Hours

A survey of adults showed that the number of hours the average adult spent working has increased since 1973. This is putting pressure on everyone, particularly on working mothers. The following table shows how many hours adults spent at work, doing housekeeping or studying, including travel time to and from a job or school.

YEAR	NUMBER OF HOURS
1973	40.6
1980	46.9
1993	50.0
1998	49.9

[Source: Inc. Magazine]

107

FACTS

PUBLIC / PRIVATE EFFORTS - DALLAS EXAMPLE:

In 1994, in response to an initiative by Dallas business leaders, some 105 companies became charter participants of the Dallas Women's Covenant. They agreed to participate in an effort to expand opportunities for women for five years. Each company was asked to set goals, measure progress, and report their results annually to the Covenant. More than 65% of the original companies have reported in each of the last four years. The areas set as **priorities for action, measurement and improvement** were:

- **Procurement from women-owned businesses;**
- **The hiring and advancement of women; and**
- **Women placements in newly-filled management and professional positions and on Corporate Boards.**

Results: **In procurement,** the total purchases from women-owned firms reported in dollars **rose more than one third between 1994 and 1997. Hiring and advancement of women for all reporting companies either remained stable or rose**. Although gains were not dramatic, women consistently made up approximately 50% of new hires. **The number of women placed** in newly-filled management and professional positions varies, with yearly gains as high as 14% some years while remaining stable in other years. Additionally, since 1994, **fifteen women have been appointed to Boards of Directors of participating companies.**

Benchmarking: In addition to, and just as important as, numerical results, **the Covenant has resulted in benchmarking by companies of the practices that have best helped them achieve the goals of the Covenant.** They have shared those Best Practices and a summary is available in the report of the program. That report is available from the Greater Dallas Chamber, 1201 Elm Street, Suite 2000, Dallas, Texas 75270, (214) 746-6728, www.dallaschamber.com.

108

CHAPTER 6: ORGANIZATIONS & NETWORKING

WOW! Top 20 Business Women's Organizations by Membership:

American Nurses Association	180,000
American Association of University Women	160,000
National Association of Female Executives	150,000
American Business Women's Association	80,000
Business and Professional Women/USA	70,000
National Council of Negro Women	55,000
American Agri-Women	50,000
Soroptimist International of the Americas	50,000
Int'l Association of Administrative Professionals	40,000
Zonta International	35,000
Women, Inc.	30,000
National Association of Colored Women's Clubs	20,000
Coalition of Labor Union Women	20,000
National Association of Working Women, 9to5	15,000
National Society of Women Engineers	14,000
National Association of Insurance Women	13,000
Women's Council of Realtors	13,000
American Medical Women's Association	13,000
Women in Film	12,000
The International Alliance	10,000

[Source: The Business Women's Network Directory, 5th Edition]

WOW! *The 1998-99 Business Women's Network (BWN) Directory* **profiles more than 1,450 women's organizations and over 850 women's Web sites.** Watch for more than 3,200 listings in October 1999, and 4,000 by October 2000!

WOW! The *BWN Directory* shows an **increase of 200% in organizations and Web sites dedicated to working mothers.**

WOW! **45% of the BWN organizations listed in the 1998-99 Directory have Web sites,** compared to only 25% in the 1997-98 edition. Some 200 of these women's organizations operate solely through the Internet, a 25% increase from 1997.

WOW! Networking is the **strongest approach to a job search,** according to the Robert Half Associates Survey of 1400 chief information officers.

WOW! **65% of women's organizations** queried **said networking was their number one goal** and number one resource for members.

WOW! The networking opportunities made available through **women's business associations are an important career builder.**

110

FACTS

WOW! __Top Five Reasons for Women to Network__: *What Professional and Business Women are Telling BWN:.*

1. Networking builds sales profitability.
2. Networking is a cost-effective way to market a business.
3. Networking is free advertising in its purest form, word of mouth.
4. Networking is a catalyst for introducing and linking people to those in need of their service who may later return the favor.
5. Everyone is a potential customer or a lead to a potential customer.

WOW! **NETWORKING WEB SITES** - Examples from thousands provided by BWN:

- **The Small Business Administration Office of Women's Business Ownership** www.sba.gov
- **National Association For Female Executives,** www.nafe.com
- **The American Business Women's Association,** www.abwahq.org
- **Business and Professional Women/USA and Foundation** www.bpwusa.org
- **American Woman's Economic Development Corporation** www.womenconnect.com/awed
- **National Association of Women Business Owners** www.nawbo.org
- **Women Inc.,** www.womeninc.com
- **iVillage.com: The Women's Network,** www.ivillage.com/company – This site offers advice and solutions for career women in a variety of communities.
- **Women's Wire: Small Business Smarts,** www.womenswire.com This site assists in the process in creating business plans for small businesses.

111

- **An Income of Her Own,** www.anincomeofherown.com
  This site provides young women with the resources needed to ensure a successful future.
- **Electra Pages,** http://electrapages.com
  This site features a comprehensive list of women's organizations.
- **Advancing Women,** www.advancingwomen.com
- **The Executive Woman's Travel Network,** www.delta-air.com/womenexecs
- **Feminist Majority Foundation,** www.feminist.org
- **National Organization for Women (NOW),** www.now.org
- **The Financial Women's Association of New York (FWA),** www.fwa.org
- **Women in Technology International (WITI),** www.witi.com
- **Women.com,** www.women.com
- **Women-Connect-Asia,** www.women-connect-asia.com
- **Womenconnect.com,** www.womenconnect.com

Note:
- **17% of web sites provides networking, social interaction and support groups.**
- **13% of web sites provide training / support for women entrepreneurs**
- **6% of web sites provide support for women's leadership.**
- **13% of women's web sites are for international support organizations**
- **28% of web sites provide local networking opportunities.**

112

CHAPTER 7: MENTORING

WOW! **In 1996 the American Society for Training and Development polled Fortune 500 companies and others on the subject of mentoring.** Their data provides insights into the uses and effectiveness of mentoring. It includes:

- **71% of Fortune 500** and other private companies **said that in their organization mentoring is used as a training tool.**

- **91% of executives credit mentoring as an important development tool; 81% claim that mentoring played a key role in their career success.**

- **7% of corporate executives report that formal internal mentoring programs have been implemented** in their company. They also state that they find that mentoring increases both retention of employees and improvement in the employees' performance.

- **Mentoring programs help to build a more loyal and effective workforce, thus saving money.** (Recruiting and training costs, on average, for a new employee are $150,000 over a three-year period.)

WOW! **Dial-A-Mentor**, a program run by the Small Business Administration's Office of Women Business Ownership (OWBO), **is a resource for women who are looking for advice and mentors.** The program matches established women business owners with those who are

113

just starting out. Contact your local SBA office or call **1-800-A-ASK-SBA** for details.

WOW! **Training and mentoring young women is a primary focus of many programs.** Examples are:

- **The Washington Center for Internships and Academic Seminars**--an independent, nonprofit educational organization founded in 1975. One of the primary and most successful programs is its Women's Leadership Program. (800) 486-8921 or www.twc.edu .

- **Girls Inc.** develops educational programs for girls age 6-18. Mentoring is a strong component of the programs for adolescents. For information call (212) 689-1253.

- **An Income of Her Own** offers a powerful entrepreneurial program for high school girls. The youth put together their own business plan. (800) 350-1816.

- **Camp Start Up** is a two-week residential teen entrepreneurial skills-building program. (800) 350-1816.

- **The Financial Women's Association of New York and the International Alliance have supported Daughters 2002** with mentoring, seminars and workshops. (212) 533-2141.

WOW! **Many women's organizations' sponsor mentoring and support programs**. There are hundreds of such programs, including the following examples:

114

FACTS

American Association of University Women Educational Foundation (AAUWEF), (202) 785-7700. The AAUW Educational Foundation awards nearly $3 million annually to more than 300 women working on postgraduate degrees.

American Business Women's Foundation (800) 361-6621 The ABW Foundation administers funds to help women achieve business goals and to promote the improvement of the business environment for women nationwide. The Foundation's Partners for Success mentoring model was developed to help previous welfare recipients overcome obstacles and stay in the work force.

American Society of Women Accountants (ASWA), (800) 326-2163. The American Society of Women Accountants was formed to increase the opportunities for women in all fields of accounting. ASWA supports The Educational Foundation of AWSCPA-ASWA. Chapters are involved with Children's Miracle Network Telethon, Public Television Auctions and Girl Scouts.

Association for Women in Science (AWIS), (202) 326-8940. The Association for Women in Science recently completed a three-year, $400,000 mentoring program funded by the Alfred P. Sloan Foundation. The Program was designed to encourage and retain female undergraduate and graduate students in the sciences.

Association of Real Estate Women (AREW), (212) 265-4652. The AREW Charitable Fund, Inc. underwrites scholarships for undergraduate and graduate students in real estate and urban studies programs at Columbia and New York Universities. Their philanthropic activities also include Women in Need, Inc. (WIN), which provides services to needy women and children.

Committee of 200, (312) 751-3477. The C200 Foundation sponsors annual university outreach seminars for women graduates, business

115

school students and emerging entrepreneurs. The Foundation also provides money for the education of young women and manages "To Mentor Our Own," a member-to-member mentoring program.

Educational Foundation for Women in Accounting, (610) 407-9229. This foundation seeks to support the advancement of women in the accounting profession through the funding of education, research, career literature, publications and other projects. The Foundation awards scholarships to women pursuing accounting degrees at the undergraduate and postgraduate levels.

Ewing Marion Kauffman Foundation, (816) 932-1221. The Kauffman Fellow Program provides firsthand experience in the venture capital process for exceptional women and men. Fellows are asked to share their knowledge with their communities through relevant programs and activities.

Hispanic Women's Corporation (HWC), (602) 954-7995. The Hispanic Women's Corporation utilizes over 200 volunteers annually to plan and deliver programs designed to empower Hispanic women through education and personal and professional development.

Karla Scherer Foundation, (312) 943-9191. The Karla Scherer Foundation is a privately-funded foundation offering scholarships to female students majoring in finance or economics who demonstrate financial need., and may become tomorrow's business leaders .

WINGS-Women in New Growth Stages, (614) 888-4674. WINGS facilitates women in all stages of their lives to participate in unique mentoring and learning opportunities via the Wind Beneath My Wings mentoring program. The WINGS Scholarship Fund helps women to transition into the workforce, or prepare for advancement, by providing tuition for college or professional development programs, and funds for supportive services such as childcare and transportation.

CHAPTER 8: CONFERENCES AND AWARDS

WOW! The Business Women's Network (BWN) has profiled more than **1,000 women's events throughout the United States.** Of the first 450 events profiled by BWN, 175 attract more than 500 attendees; 300 host 1,000 or more attendees.

WOW! **Professional Development and Careers is the number one category for women's events,** garnering a total of 24% of the events listed in the BWN Calendar of Key Women's Events.

WOW! **The Top 6 Women's Conferences are:**

- Governor of California's "A Call to Women": 9,000
- National Conference of State Legislatures-Women's Network:: 7,500
- Wired to Win: Leading Edge Technologies for Women: 7,000
- National Association for Girls & Women in Sports - Centennial Celebration: 6,000
- Business and Professional Women (BPW): 6,000
- Women Mean Business: Global Exchange: 1,000

WOW! **The Top 5 popular states** for women's events are:

- California: 11.6%
- District of Columbia: 9.4%
- New York: 9.1%
- Illinois: 6.1%
- Arizona: 3.9%

117

AWARDS FOR WOMEN

WOW! **Recognition is basic to the success of women's programs.**
BWN has profiled more than 1,500 groups. The numbers of awards and
recognition programs, and the scope and breath of women's recognition
program and awards are impressive.

WOW! CORPORATE AWARDS

There are three primary examples of awards made by companies to
outstanding women entrepreneurs on the basis of leadership.

AVON WOMEN OF ENTERPRISE AWARD: The Avon Women of
Enterprise Awards are twelve years old in 1999. They are partnership
between Avon and the Small Business Administration (SBA). **Each year
the program pays tribute to six dynamic women** who have overcome
professional and often personal obstacles to become some of the most
successful entrepreneurs. www.avon.com/about/women/move/history.

BANK ONE ENTREPRENEURIAL AWARDS PROGRAM: With
Working Woman's Entrepreneurial Award, sponsored by Bank One, is
an awards program that encompasses both regional and national successes
by female entrepreneurs. In addition, the events provide a meeting ground
where networking and idea-sharing can occur. The award divisions are:
**fastest growing, innovation, best employer, overcoming obstacles,
turnaround situation, socially responsible, customer/client service and
general excellence.**

SARA LEE FRONTRUNNER AWARDS. This award was created to
celebrate the accomplishments of women and to provide inspiration for
others. Sara Lee Frontrunners are national innovators and leaders in their

118

fields. **The different areas of recognition are the arts, business, government and the humanities.**

![WOW!] We estimate that thousands of awards are presented each year by women's organizations. ATHENA, for example, gives an award in more than 400 communities for leadership and support of women. **The awards we highlight are exemplary, but are only a sampling of those presented annually by women's groups across the country.**

American Agri-Women (AAW), (724) 458-6108: AAW presents the **Leaven Awards** to members who make outstanding contributions to the organization and to agriculture. Nominees are judged on the following qualities: loyalty, enthusiasm, anticipation, strength, effectiveness and nurturing.

American Bar Association: Commission on Women in the Profession, (312) 988-5668: The American Bar Association Commission on Women in the Profession awards the **Margaret Brent Women Lawyers of Achievement Award**. The award recognizes and celebrates the accomplishments of women lawyers.

American Business Women's Association (ABWA), (816) 361-6621: ABWA recognizes ten members as the **Top Ten Business Women of ABWA** each year. From these women, one is chosen as the American Business Woman of ABWA. Winners are recognized at the Association's national convention, in *Women in Business Magazine* and often receive national press coverage.

American Women in Radio and Television (AWRT), (703) 506-3290: AWRT presents such awards as the **Gracie Allen Awards** recognizing outstanding television programming that realistically portrays women. The **Silver Satellite Awards**, which are given for outstanding accomplishments in the field of electronic communications, and **the Star Awards**, which are

119

granted to three individuals and three companies on the basis of their sensitivity and commitment to the concerns of women.

Association for Women in Communications, (410) 544-7442: The Association for Women in Communications presents several awards for excellence in communication and dedication to the organization. These awards are the **Clarion Awards**, the **Headliner Award**, the **Rising Star Award**, the **Georgina MacDougall Davis Award** and the **Chairman's First Women in Communications Award.**

Association for Women in Computing, (415) 905-4663: The Association for Women in Computing awards the **Augusta Ada Lovelace Award** to a woman of outstanding accomplishment in the field of computing.

Association for Women in Mathematics, (301) 405-7892: The Association for Women in Mathematics awards **the Alice T. Schafer Award** to a female student for outstanding undergraduate work and the **Louise Hay Award** for excellence in mathematics education. It also hosts the Emmy Noether Lectures, which honor women who have made fundamental and sustained contributions to the mathematical sciences.

Association for Women in Science (AWIS), (202) 326-8940: The AWIS Educational Foundation **awards grants of $500 to $1000** to female students earning a doctorate degree in any life, physical or social science or engineering program.

ATHENA Foundation, (800) 548-8247: ATHENA Awards are given to individuals recognized for professional achievement and community service and for actively and generously assisting women in their attainment of professional excellence and leadership skills. Men and women are eligible to receive the Award. The **ATHENA State Award** honors companies and institutions for their professional accomplishments, community service and for their unique initiatives to provide leadership opportunities for women.

FACTS

Business and Professional Women USA (BPW/USA), (202) 293-1100: The **Women Mean Business Award Gala** honors exceptional women who make contributions to business and workplace equity.

Catalyst, (212) 514-7600: **The Catalyst Awards** honor up to three individuals, corporations or professional firms that have undertaken to advance women in the workplace. Initiatives considered include programs or systematic practices that promote women's leadership and career development.

Connecticut Women's Hall of Fame, (860) 675-8242: The Connecticut Women's Hall of Fame has an annual Award Induction Ceremony and Celebration to honor its inductees.

Cosmetic Executive Women, Inc., (212) 759-3283: **The Cosmetic Executive Women Beauty Awards** recognize outstanding creativity and innovation in the beauty industry in seven categories. The annual **Achiever Award** honors a leading woman executive who has contributed significantly to the beauty industry and the community.

Enterprising Women's Leadership Institute (EWLI), (518) 465-5579: **The Golden Leadership Recognition Awards** Reception recognizes state, regional and local organizations that have promoted women to senior leadership positions.

Entrepreneurial Mothers Association, (602) 899-5116: Each chapter of EMA **awards the Entrepreneurial Mother of the Year Award**, recognizing a member for outstanding accomplishments in her business and professional life.

The Fashion Group, (212) 593-1715: The Fashion Group's Night of Stars honors outstanding women and men. Past honorees include Donna Karan, Karl Lagerfeld and Diane Sawyer.

121

Financial Women's Association of New York (FWANY), (212) 533-2141: An annual awards dinner honors the **"Woman of the Year"** for significant professional achievement. Awards are presented to one public sector honoree and one private sector honoree.

International Alliance for Women in Music, (724) 357-7918: **The Pauline Alderman Awards** are presented for new research on women in music. The prize-winning research projects have included books, articles, papers, essays, dissertations and other published and unpublished materials.

International Federation of Women's Travel Organizations (IFWTO), (602) 596-6640: IFWTO presents three awards at its annual convention. **The Bergen-Sullivan Tourism Award** is presented to an entity, person or company that has made an outstanding and ongoing contribution to the worldwide travel and tourism industry. **The Spirit Award** is awarded to a member who has contributed outstanding service to the Federation. **The Susan Thomas Memorial Award** is presented to the outstanding club of the year.

MANA, A National Latina Organization, (202) 833-0060: MANA's **"Las Primeras"** is a recognition program that honors women of achievement who are firsts in their fields and role models for younger Latinas.

National Association for Girls and Women in Sports (NAGWS), (703) 476-3450: The NAGWS awards the **Wade Trophy** to the country's most outstanding senior collegiate female basketball player.

National Association of Home Builders Women's Council, (202) 822-0433: The Women's Council awards program is designed to recognize the achievements of local Councils and individuals in areas ranging from education to membership development. **Leadership Achievement Awards** recognize members for outstanding leadership skills through the awards, **"Woman of the Year," "Outstanding National Representative of the Year,"** and **"Outstanding Local President of the Year."**

122

National Association of Negro Business and Professional Women's Clubs, Inc. (NANBPWC), (202) 483-4206: The NANBPWC awards the Frederick Douglas Award, the National **Youth Award**, the National **Achievement** Award, the National Community Service Award, the Crystal Award, the National Appreciation Award and the Sojourner Truth Award.

National Association of Women Business Owners (NAWBO), (301) 608-2590: The NAWBO awards an honor for women who have achieved success despite personal or economic challenges and various awards for developing women entrepreneurs, **a Woman Business Owner of the Year Award, a Public Policy Advocate of the Year award and a Corporate Partner of the Year award.**

National Association of Working Women, 9to5, (414) 274-0925: 9to5 sponsors an annual Boss Contest which highlights model employers, policies and the types of treatment and conditions for working women which need to be addressed.

National Coalition of 100 Black Women (NCBW), (212) 947-2196: NCBW honors distinguished black women with **the Candace Award.**

National Federation of Black Women Business Owners (NFBWBO), (202) 833-3450: NFBWBO hosts the **Annual Black Women Business Awards** which honor "Black Women of Courage."

National Women's Hall of Fame, (315) 568-8060: **The Hall of Fame** honors distinguished American women with induction into the Hall. They are chosen for the value of their contribution to society, to significant groups within society, and to the progress and freedom of women; their contributions to art, athletics, business, government, philanthropy, humanities, science and education; and the enduring value of their achievements.

123

Professional Businesswomen of California (PBWC), (650) 548-2424: An annual **"Breakthrough Award"** is presented to a professional woman who exemplifies excellence and is making significant contributions to business and the community.

Soroptimist International of the Americas (SIA), (800) 942-4629: SIA's **Women's Opportunity Awards** assist women who serve as the primary breadwinners for their families to offset any costs associated with attaining higher education and additional skills training. **Women of Distinction Awards** honor women who have made outstanding achievements in their professional, business or voluntary activities. **Advancing the Status of Women Awards** are given to businesses and organizations that advance the status of women and promote women's issues.

SBA, Francis Perkins Vanguard Award, (877) 722-3263: This award honors government and industry for their excellence in use of women owned small businesses as prime contractors and subcontractors. The SBA's Office of Government Contracting determines the finalists.

Texas Executive Women, (713) 507-2180: Texas Executive Women co-sponsor **"Women on the Move."** In the course of this ongoing project, more than one hundred women have been honored for their achievements and contributions.

Wider Opportunities for Women, (202) 638-3143: Women at Work Awards honor leaders ranging from communications to working women. These awards include **the Commissioner's Award, the Entertainment Award, the Broadcast Journalism Award, the Public Policy Award, the Workplace Initiative Award, and the Individual Leadership Award.**

The Women's Business Enterprise National Council (WBENC), (202) 862-4810. WBENC introduced its APPLAUSE_ Awards Program in March of 1999. The program recognizes and "applauds" the "barrier breakers" who expand business opportunities for women business owners with a

124

significant first time ever contribution that furthers the mission of WBENC. Corporations, women business owners, government agencies and/or individuals are eligible to receive this award. The APPLAUSE_ Award is not an annual award; it will be awarded whenever a significant act occurs which advances business opportunities for women.

Women Executives in Public Relations (WEPR), (203) 226-4947: WEPR hosts an Awards for Social Responsibility Luncheon, at which the Foundation recognizes the efforts of individuals and organizations for making unique social contributions to such areas as human rights, the environment, health, education, culture, employment or homelessness.

Women Executives in State Government (WESG), (202) 628-9374: WESG presents the **"Breaking the Glass Ceiling" Awards**, which recognize individuals who are making strides to shatter the invisible barrier to advancement in the workplace. Awards are presented to four persons: a Governor, a person in the public sector, a person in the private sector and a woman in state government.

Women in Cable and Telecommunications (WICT), (312) 634-2330: WICT hosts an annual awards breakfast recognizing industry leaders and organizations that have furthered the goals of the organization. These awards include **"Woman of the Year,"** which is presented to a woman who has made a significant contribution to the industry in the past year, and "Woman to Watch," which is presented to a young woman with leadership potential who exhibits job excellence as well as strong dedication to the industry.

Women in Engineering Programs and Advocates Network (WEPAN), (765) 494-5387: WEPAN presents three awards: **The President's Award, the WEPAN Research Award and the Women in Engineering Program Award**. The President's Award honors an individual who has demonstrated a significant contribution. The WEPAN Research Award notes achievement in research related to women in engineering and science. The

125

WIE Program Award is awarded to a college or university program judged to have made significant advances as a start-up program within its first year of existence.

Women in Film (WIF), (213) 463-6040: WIF presents the **Crystal Awards Luncheon**, an event which honors the lifetime achievements of entertainment professionals, and the **Lucy Awards Luncheon**, which acknowledge television trailblazers who exemplify the extraordinary achievements of Lucille Ball.

Women in Production (WIP), (212) 481-7793: The **Luminaire Award** recognizes the outstanding achievements and personal dedication of women and men in the graphic arts industry.

Women's Foodservice Forum, (630) 262-9992: The **Emerging Leader Award** honors an emerging woman leader in the food service and hospitality industries.

Women's Funding Network (WFN), (651) 227-1911: WFN recognizes women leaders with **the "Changing the Face of Philanthropy Awards.** Each honoree provides leadership in the women's funding movement by inspiring, challenging and modeling social change philanthropy.

Women's Health Executives Network (WHEN), (847) 256-4422: The **Achievement in Health Care Management Award** is presented to a woman who has demonstrated outstanding personal achievement and has promoted the advancement of women in health executive positions.

Women's International Center, (619) 295-6446: WIC bestows the **"Living Legacy Award"** for individuals who have made a great difference in the world. Winners demonstrate a focused vision, plan and willingness to seek truth beauty, greatness and generosity that affects other women, children and men across the world.

126

WOW! Women Who Have Recently Won the Nobel Prize:

Jody Williams① (US)	Peace	1997
C. Nüsslein-Volhard② (Germany)	Physics/Medicine	1995
Toni Morrison (US)	Literature	1993
Rigoberta Menchu (Guatemala)	Peace	1992
Nadine Gordiner (South Africa)	Literature	1991
Aung San Su Kyi (Myanmar)	Peace	1991
Gertrude Ellinson③ (US)	Physics/Medicine	1988
Rita Levi-Montaleini④ (Italy)	Physics/Medicine	1986
Barbara McClintock (US)	Physics/Medicine	1983
Mother Theresa (Macedonia)	Peace	1979

① Shared with International Campaign to Ban Landmines.
② Shared with two men.③ Shared with two men.④ Shared with a man.

[Source: The Top 10 of Everything, DK Publishing]

WOW! Corporations are celebrating their achievements.
For Example – KPMG is proud of the following awards:
- 100 Best Companies to Work For. (Business Week, 1997)
- Highest Percentage of Female Partners (Bowman's 1998)
- Diversity Front Runner. (CPA Personnel Report, 1998)

WOW! Awards and Recognition

Each day recognition is made of top women. Switzerland elected its first woman President in 1999. (Switzerland did not even give women suffrage until 1971.)

127

WOW! FACTS™

CHAPTER 9: PHILANTHROPY & COMMUNITY INVOLVEMENT

WOW! Women are the philanthropic decision-makers in 32% of American households.

WOW! The average annual charitable contribution made by women increased by 26% from 1993 to 1996. During that same time span the rise in contributions **by men was only 6%** according to a survey by Independent Sector of Washington, DC.

WOW! Women donate 1.8% of their annual income, on average, while **men donate 3.1% of income**.

WOW! Women volunteer more! 64% of women volunteer, compared to only 45% of men.

WOW! In philanthropic organizations, women hold over 50% of the CEO positions.

WOW! Women expect results when they make philanthropic contributions according to a survey conducted by the Women's Funding Network of St. Paul, Minnesota.

The following BWN Survey indicates the percentage of women's organizations surveyed that have as a key purpose a focus on: **networking, volunteering, mentorship, giving recognition to women leaders and offering scholarship to students and entrepreneurs.**

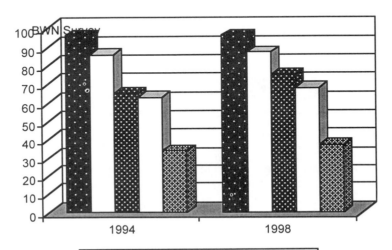

FACTS

PHILANTHROPIC INITIATIVES

WOW! "Call it patronage with a personal touch. Executive and managerial women are looking for new ways to make their voices heard – and their money mean something – in the philanthropic arena.** Driven by mounting disposable incomes and the desire to give, and in some cases, to shine a brighter spotlight on themselves or their companies, they are no longer content just to shoot a check into the mail or buy tickets to the annual charity ball! **They want to take action themselves.**" *[Annetta Miller and Seema Nayyar, Working Woman, July/August 1998]*

The examples below illustrate just a **few of the many innovative and effective approaches that women are taking to philanthropic giving**.

WOW! **The Dress for Success** program was begun in New York City by a young woman, Nancy Lublin, with a $5,000 inheritance that she wanted to use to help others. With the support of retailers she began to **provide unemployed women with suits and dresses "suitable"** for use during job interviews. In New York City where the program was begun less than two years ago, more than 1,200 women have received clothing. The program has expanded to Boston, Cleveland, New Orleans and St. Louis. They have also **expanded their goals and plan to begin a support group for women who have just entered the job market.** Dress for Success Worldwide; (212) 989-6373.

WOW! **The Susan Koman Breast Cancer Foundation was begun in 1982 by her sister Nancy Brinker.** With efforts like their "Ultimate Drive," the groups raise millions of dollars annually and is now the **largest private funding source for breast cancer research.** (877) 4A-DRIVE.

131

WOW! The <u>Ms. Foundation for Women</u> from New York City (not connected with *Ms. Magazine*) provides **a resource for women interested in "hands on" philanthropy that is often aimed at making systemic changes rather than simply giving to the needy**. The group uses **funding circles and collaboratives, scholarship programs, grants and internships.** Their programs are aimed at **women who want some involvement in their philanthropic efforts but cannot devote full time to them.** The collaborative groups they form work to pool contributions, review requests for grants, and visit applicants. The group then chooses the project to which they will contribute. In Philadelphia, for example, a collaborative group of 20 women each donate $25,000 a year and work together to decide how to "spend" it. **The Foundation also educates donors about women's' issues.** Call (212) 742-2300 for more information.

WOW! <u>Welfare to Work programs</u> have sprung up in Washington, DC, Atlanta, GA, Philadelphia, PA, Dallas, TX, and Los Angeles, CA. These businesses are helping to train and hire women to become self-sufficient and instill confidence and pride. **Women business owners have pledged to provide more than 13,000 jobs** to help get women off welfare. For further information call (202) 955-3005.

WOW! Contact BWN and others for women's conferences on **philanthropy. Examples:** Women's Funding Network session called "Women and Girls are the Future of a Just Society: Innovative Strategies in Philanthropy. Contact the Women's Funding Network for more information. (651) 227-1911.

WOW! It is estimated that **30% of women's organizations,** according to Edie Fraser, President of the Business Women's Network (BWN), **are**

supporting philanthropic programs such as scholarships, special grants, and community involvement. *Working Mother Magazine* started "Daughters 2002". Supportive groups include the Financial Women's Association, The International Alliance, the National Association for Female Executives (NAFE), the National Association of Women Business Owners (NAWBO) and the American Association of University Women (AAUW).

PHILANTHROPIC ORGANIZATION EXAMPLES

Altrusa National, Inc., (312) 427-4410. Altrusa National has administered contributions of more than $3 million to help members meet pressing human needs. Their programs include the ABC Literacy Grants Program, the Anniversary Gift Campaign and the Diamond Jubilee Endowment Fund.

Association of Junior Leagues International (AJLI), (212) 393-3364. AJLN is a national organization of women committed to promoting volunteerism and to improving the community through the effective action of trained volunteers.

Black Women Organized for Educational Development (BWOED), (510) 763-9501. BWOED implements programs that improve and maintain the socioeconomic well-being of women in transition. They provide a mentoring program that educates students on such issues as teen pregnancy, HIV, substance abuse and violence. BWOED offers free legal advice on wills, probate, personal injury, real estate, family law and other civil areas.

Boston Women's Fund (BWF), (617) 725-0035. The Boston Women's Fund is a fund that links people who have resources with women who have ideas and solutions. The organization focuses on allocating grants to needed areas from the money they raise.

Chicago Foundation for Women (CFW), (312) 266-1176. The Chicago Foundation for Women provides grants to nonprofit organizations led by and serving women and girls, attempts to bring together grantees and

133

funders to discuss relevant issues, provides technical training and assistance to grantees on women's issues and co-sponsors community events and projects that focus on women's issues.

Dallas Women's Foundation, (214) 965-9977. The Dallas Women's Foundation has given more than $1.7 million to agencies and programs that promote the areas of basic needs, economics, education, health, social/legal, math, science and technology for women and girls. The organization's major fundraising events are an annual luncheon and the Circle of Honor Tribute Dinner.

Links, The, (202) 842-8686. The Links Incorporated, is an organization of African-American women that has granted more than $10 million to such charitable organizations as The United College Fund/UNCF, The National Urban League, The National Merit Achievement Foundation and Dance Theater of Harlem.

Los Angeles Women's Foundation (LAWF), (213) 938-9828. The LAWF provides funding, training and management assistance to community-based organizations that meet the needs of low-income and under served women and girls throughout Los Angeles County. The Foundation provides grants in organizational development, program development and
new projects in the areas of violence against women, economic justice for women, women's health and self-determination of girls and young women.

National Association of Working Women, 9to5, (414) 274-0925. 9to5, National Association of Working Women, is a membership and advocacy organization. The mission is to improve the pay and status of working women with a primary focus on women office workers. **9to5's Job Retention Program** offers training and support for women receiving public assistance to help them attain financial self-sufficiency. **9to5** also offers the Sexual Harassment Outreach and Education Program (SHOEP).

New Mexico Women's Foundation, (505) 268-3996. The New Mexico Women's Foundation identifies critical and emerging areas affecting the lives of women in the State of New Mexico. Volunteers, board members and donors work together on programs that help women achieve their goals.

New York Women's Foundation, (212) 226-2220. The New York Women's Foundation funds programs within the five boroughs of New York City which contribute to moving low-income women and girls toward economic self-sufficiency by serving their employment, education, child care, housing or health care needs. The Foundation initiated the program "Growing Girls," which emphasizes positive development of girls between the ages of nine and fifteen.

Soroptimist International of the Americas (SIA), (800) 942-4629 or (215) 557-9300. SIA is one of four federations that focus on economic and social development, education, environment, health, human rights/ status of women and international goodwill and understanding.

Stephen Bufton Memorial Education Fund (816) 361-6621 is the national scholarship trust of the American Business Women's Association. Created in 1956, the fund has awarded over $12 million to help women achieve their professional and personal goals and keep pace with the changing demands of the workplace.

Women's Charities of America (WCA), (800) 626-6481. The WCA pre-screens high quality national and international charities and presents them to potential givers in fund drives at work and on the web.

Women in Community Service (WICS), (703) 671-0500. WICS volunteers and staff help more than 150,000 low-income women and young adults annually by providing support services, mentoring and work force preparation programs nationwide. WICS participates in such national events as "Make a Difference Day" and "National Youth Services Day."

135

© Business Women's Network, Washington, DC 20036
(800) 48-WOMEN
http://www.bwni.com

Women's Funding Network (WFN), (651) 227-1911. WFN recognizes women leaders with the "Changing the Face of Philanthropy Awards." Each of the honorees provides leadership in the women's funding movement by inspiring, challenging and modeling social change philanthropy.

Women and Philanthropy, (202) 887-9660. Women and Philanthropy is an association of grantmakers who focus on the welfare of women and girls.

Women's Philanthropy Institute (WPI), (608) 286-0980. The WPI brings together philanthropists and philanthropy professionals to educate and advance women as major donors and volunteer leaders for the nonprofit causes and institutions of their choosing. WPI's National Speakers Bureau provides speakers for donor events and professional activities.

Women's Foundation of Colorado, (303) 832-8800. The Women's Foundation of Colorado has awarded nearly $1.6 million to 131 programs that focus on employment and training to assist the most at-risk women and girls. They developed and funded the special initiative "Girls Count" and continue to fund programs addressing the needs of women and girls of all ethnic, racial and economic backgrounds.

YWCA of the USA, (212) 273-7800. The YWCA is the largest and oldest women's organization in the United States. They are the leading provider of shelter and services to women and their families, providing shelter to more than 650,000 people each year. The YWCA provides child care for 750,000 children in over 1000 sites in the United States and trains 8000 childcare providers and 7000 babysitters each year.

Zonta International, (312) 930-5848. Zonta is a service organization with a heavy focus on community involvement. Some of their projects include contributing voluntary service dollars to build health and education centers in Columbia, adopting the Pan African Training and Research Center for Women in cooperation with UNICEF and providing mobile pediatric units.

136

CHAPTER 10: WELFARE TO WORK

WOW! The Small Business Administration has been supported by many women's organizations, women entrepreneurs, and corporate America in the hiring and training of women who want to be in control of their own lives and move from welfare to a business environment. Thousands are pledging and hiring women – with great results.

WOW! The U.S. Departments of Labor, Commerce, and Education have launched initiatives to help match U.S. workers with high-tech job opportunities and to move information technology companies toward e-commerce:

WOW! Welfare to Work is a priority for women. SBA, Welfare to Work Partnership, the Business Women's Network (BWN), and others have focused on hundreds of thousands of jobs.

WOW! BWN with SBA committed hiring 12,000 women with commitments from women entrepreneurs. The National Association of Women Business Owners(NAWBO), is the leading organization that has committed the most jobs with 8,000. On September 10, 1997, at the National Press Club, BWN's pledge campaign of hiring welfare workers was showcased. SBA (202) 205-6706 web: www.sba.gov/w2w, BWN (800)-48 WOMEN www.bwni.com

WOW! Women in New Growth Stages (WINGS): WINGS joined the pledge campaign, for example. "Establish a nurturing, learning environment

137

that facilitates women's transitions in life and the workplace…" This is the basis from which WINGS of Columbus, OH., founded its organization in 1995. The results have been significant—obtaining jobs, pursuing higher education, increased community involvement. (614) 888-4674. www.wings-women.com

WOW! **Alliance of Business Women International (ABWI): ABWI** is running a special welfare to work program for the state of New Mexico which should be a model for other states. 1 (800) 606-2294

WOW! **WICS challenges women business owner to "Take Two to Work."** WICS is advocating that each woman-owned firm hire two qualified welfare recipients. Working with women of poverty since 1964, WICS provides volunteer mentors and the support necessary for the successful transition into the workplace. (703) 671-0500. www.WICS.org

WOW! **Welfare to Work Partnership** was launched on May 20, 1997, at the White House. This national non-partisan not-for-profit was formed to help businesses hiring individuals from public assistance. The partnership is focused on hiring through small, medium and large companies hiring former welfare recipients. Call for further information: (202) 955-3005. www.welfaretowork.crg

WOW! **Many other organizations are showing commitment and action programs.**

138

WOW! FACTS

Examples:

- **Career Action Center of Palo Alto, CA through the University of CA Placement program.**

- **Coalition for Women's Economic Development of Los Angeles. CWED provides leadership for self-employment and micro-business ownership.**

- **Women's Economic Growth (WEG), of Weed, CA. WEG serves several thousand clients and employers to employ full and part-time workers for economic independence.**

- **Women Unlimited (WU), of Augusta ME. WU is dedicated to expanding non-traditional employment options offering direct training and advocacy.**

- **Women's Initiative for Self-Employment Program of Ann Arbor Community Development Program** has an incentive program to empower low income women

WOW! **The Urban Institute** (202) 833-7200, found that welfare mothers, typically the family bread winners for the nearly four million families receiving assistance, have over four years of work experience. The average age of the adult recipients is 31 years and families receiving cash assistance have an average of two children. Welfare recipients are from racially and ethnically diverse backgrounds:

- 36% are white.
- 37% are African-American.
- 21% are Hispanic.

139

CHAPTER 11: POLITICS AND GOVERNMENT

WOW! 45 women around the world have become Presidents or Prime Ministers; 25 have done so since 1990.

WOW! There are **65 women in the 106th Congress.** Nine are senators and 56 are representatives.

WOW! In 1992 the "Year of the Woman" there was a **70% increase in the number of women in Congress-from 32 to 54.**

WOW! In 1969, women held just 4 percent of all state legislative seats in the country. In every two-year election cycle since then, that percentage has risen: to 10.3% in 1979, to 20.5% in 1993 and to **22.3% today. There are 1,652 women legislators in 1999.**

WOW! There are seven women governors of states. Arizona has become the first state in the nation where women hold the five top elected positions, including the governership which is held by Jane Hull.

141

WOW! Prominent women's political organizations and Web sites include these examples:

- **National Foundation for Women Legislators (NFWL):** NFWL is the first and only individual membership organization for present and former women legislators. NFWL is a non-partisan, nonprofit educational foundation consisting of members of the National Order of Women Legislators and corporate and associate members (women and men). Contact: Phone # (202) 337-3565; or E-mail - nfwl@erols.com

- **National Women's Political Caucus (NWPC):** NWPC is a national, grassroots organization dedicated to increasing the number of women in elected and appointed office at all levels of government, regardless of any party affiliation, bipartisan and pro-choice. Contact: (202) 785-3605; or visit their Web site at www.nwpc.org.

- **Project VOTE SMART:** The site provides information about candidates and elected officials, state and federal government, issues and historical documents. Visit their Web site www.vote.smart.org.

- **Women in Politics:** A quarterly journal that focuses on explaining the place of women in politics. For information call: 1 (888) 836-6504, or visit their Web site: www.wesstga.edu/-wandplwtp.

- **Women Legislator's Lobby (WLL) :** WLL is a bipartisan national membership program initiated by WAND (Women's Action for New Directions). It is the only organization of women state legislators working to influence the formulation of federal laws, policies, and budget priorities. Contact: (202) 543-8505; or visit their Web site at www.wand.org.

- **Women's Campaign Fund (WCF):** As the Women's Campaign Fund approaches its 25th anniversary, the group believes that adding to the ranks of women holding office has never been more of a priority. In 1998, WCF supported more progressive women candidates than any other national organization, bipartisan and pro-choice. Contact: (202) 393-8164 or visit their Web site www.womenconnect.com/wcf.

- **Womenconnect.com (WCC):** Political site: "**Politics Daily**." WCC has begun a political service that provides daily news briefings on women and politics from the National Journal's *Hotline*. As women have done in past elections, Womenconnect states that "women voters will have a critical impact on the outcome of the 1998 elections, and monitoring and participation are important." Visit their Web site at www.womenconnect.com.

- **White House Project:** The White House Project is a non-profit, non-partisan public awareness effort dedicated to changing American politics over the next decade. It is working to change our political climate so that qualified women from all walks of life can launch successful campaigns for the US Presidency and other key positions. The Ballot Box Initiative led to the naming by respondents of five women who they felt could serve as President of the US The five were announced in February 1999: First Lady Hillary Rodham Clinton, Elizabeth Hanford Dole, Senator Dianne Feinstein, Gen. Claudia Kennedy, and Governor Christine Todd Whitman. Contact: Marie Wilson: (212) 742-2300 or visit their Web site at www.thewhitehouseproject.com

WOW! FACTS™

CHAPTER 12: LEADERSHIP

Leadership takes vision and determination. Leadership and management go hand-in-hand. Leadership training and education are fundamental to overall success. **BWN salutes leadership and recognizes that many women's organizations are advocating leadership at every turn.** Although we particularly note the work of Leadership America, we also salute the efforts of many other organizations.

WOW! Leadership seminars and conferences are held weekly. One example is the **Women in Leadership: Valuing Differences: Maximizing Talent.** (781) 862-3157 www.linkageinc.com.

LEADING WOMEN'S ORGANIZATIONS
Examples:

- **American Association of University Women Leadership Program (AAUW), (202) 785-7700.**
  The AAUW is the nation's leading advocate for an equitable and excellent education for women and girls. AAUW presents several awards for outstanding achievement toward the organization's goals of educational equity for women and girls.

- **American Business Women's Associaton (ABWA) Leadership Program, (816) 361-6621.**
  Since its initiation in 1987, the ABWA Leadership Program has helped nearly 16,000 women develop and hone their leadership skills and gain confidence in their abilities to lead.

- **ATHENA Foundation, (808) 548-8247.**
  ATHENA Foundation works with local and state Chambers of Commerce, corporations and institutions to open the doors of leadership opportunities for women. The ATHENA Awards are given to individuals and companies for providing leadership opportunities and support for women. ATHENA will debut a new Leadership Model at the International Leadership Conference in 1999. This model is derived from the mission of the ATHENA Foundation and from the leadership priorities and practices of ATHENA Award recipients. The ATHENA Leadership Model draws on the talents of women and men inclusively, affirming a philosophy of leadership that celebrates relationships and service to the community.

- **Center for Women's Global Leadership, (732) 932-8782.**
  The Center seeks to develop an understanding of the ways in which gender affects the exercise of power and the conduct of public policy internationally. They run a two-week women's Global Leadership Institute. Visit their Web site www.feminist.com/afgl.html.

- **Leadership America, Inc., (703) 549-1102.**
  Leadership America is a national, non-profit leadership program for women of achievement that seeks to develop more women leaders and to link them to their peers around the world. www.leadershipamerica.com.

- **National Businesswomen's Leadership Association, (800) 258-7246.**
  This organization runs one-day workshops across the country.

- **National Foundation for Women Legislators, Inc., (202) 337-3565.**
  NFWL is the first and only individual membership organization for present and former women legislators.

- **Women's Leadership Program/The Washington Center, (202) 336- 7600 or (800) 486-8921.**
  The Women's Leadership Program is aimed at college students. It fosters the self-awareness and understanding of women as executives; providing opportunities for reflection, feedback, and planned development for women; and offers insights and strategies that integrate female identity with organizational realities. www. twc.edu.

- **Vanguard Foundation, (703) 803-3728.**
  This non-profit organization focuses on providing information and developing initiatives to identify and sustain leaders who will in-turn help others to advance in their profession. The Vanguard Award is presented to organizations that have made permanent changes and have implemented programs to advance women to position of influence and leadership in the workplace.

- **Women in Cable and Telecommunications, The Betty Magnes Leadership Institute, (312) 634-2330.**
  This organization focuses on issues related to the empowerment of women and workforce productivity. They run the Betsy Magnes Leadership Institute where senior and mid-level women managers take part in an intensive leadership and development program. Every January, a leadership conference is run for their members and national leaders. Visit their Web site at www.wict.org.

CHAPTER 13: GLOBAL

WOW! Leading **women entrepreneurs worldwide collectively generate $139 billion U.S. dollars in revenues and employ over 150,000 people.** Their businesses are headquartered **in 22 different countries**; 27% are in manufacturing, 25% are in retail trade, 10% are in real estate, and 18% are multi-industry conglomerates.

WOW! Around the world, **women-owned firms** typically comprise between **25% and 33% of the business population.**

WOW! The **World Association of Women Entrepreneurs (Les Femmes Chefs d'Entreprises Mondiales, FCEM);** is an active global association of women entrepreneurs in more than 30 countries. FCEM is not the only but is the largest network of women entrepreneurs in the world. FCEM has consultative status at the United Nations in New York, at the ILO in Geneva, at UNIDO in Vienna and the European Parliament in Brussels. www.fcem.org

WOW! . **The British Association of Women Entrepreneurs** is extremely strong. Within the Commonwealth there are more than 500 women's groups--the Confederation of British Industry--working together with FCEM, there is a great growth of women business owners across Europe, in particular. FCEM has a consultative status with the Council of Europe. It holds a major International Congress each year. As with the National Association of Women Business Centers, FCEM offers a directory in Britain alone. For further information contact, Arline Woutersz, fax 0171 224 0582, woutersz@msn.com.

149

WOW! **Women's Global Conferences** are attracting women for trade, entrepreneurial and networking interests, They are evident in each continent.

Examples:
- **OECD Conferences** for Women
- **CEM Global Summit**, London, 1998, with 72 countries participating. 3rd **"Leading Women of the World" Conference:** Monte Carlo, Monaco, April, 1999
- **Canada-U.S. Summit**, Toronto, May, 1999.
- **Greece Global Conference**, Athens, May, 1999.
- **Women Mean Business**: A Global Exchange, Lessons Without Borders, Chicago, June 2-3, 1999.
- Business Women's Network **Global Renaissance Conference, Washington, Oct. 1999.**
- Second China U.S. Conference on Women's Issues: "Holding up half the sky." Beijing, October 1999
- **African Summit** in 1998 and **Global Summit in Miami** for May, 2000.
- **FCEM Global Summit** , Toronto, 2000.

WOW! Women in the corporate world are **playing major roles in international trade and negotiation.**

WOW! Top executives who consider their companies to be successful globally, **spend 40% of their time on global issues,** compared with an overall 25%.

WOW! **35% of women-owned businesses with international dealings are listed on their country's stock exchange.**

150

WOW! Top external issues affecting growth and development of women-owned international businesses are:

- Government business laws and policies (86%);
- State of their country's economy (81%);
- Gaining access to technology (79%);
- Access to capital for business growth (79%);
- Infrastructure development and expansion (i.e. roads, electricity);
- Telephones (74%); and
- Political instability (70%).

WOW! There **are hundreds of global women's Web sites.** Some examples are:

- **Annuaire au Feminin**: Listing women's organizations in France;
- **FemiNet Asia**: Designed to improve the status of women in Korea, Malaysia, Mongolia, and China;
- **Women-Connect-Asia**: Announcements, articles, and business registration.

WOW! **Women business owners internationally share similar concerns about key business issues.** Women business owners in Africa, Russia and the US agree that maintaining profitability and cash flow are key concerns. (Most countries cite the same in surveys.)

WOW! **Women share common concerns worldwide.** <u>Avon's Global Woman's Survey</u> shows that women want **"greater security and control regarding family, financial and work circumstances."**

151

FACTS

The survey **included 30,000 women in 43 countries.** Data included the following:

- 57% rated the following as equally important and essential to happiness: a good family life, financial security and health;

- 75% cited work-family balance as their greatest challenge;

- 55% cited achieving financial independence as most important; and37% wanted to have a greater role in business.

COUNTRY FACTS

AFRICA

WOW! **Africa is the epitome of where women are small business owners.** All women should be proud of the African Federation of Women Entrepreneurs (AFWE). There are ten million women business owners across Africa. The African Federation has been active for a decade. In September, 1997, AFWE hosted the International Conference in Accra. AFWE organized the Second Global Women Entrepreneurs Trade Fair and Investment Forum in Addis Ababa, Ethiopia. The third will be held in Miami, summer 2000.

WOW! **Africa claims as many as 10 million women entrepreneurs and the numbers continue to grow as African women seek economic development.**

152

AUSTRALIA

Government

WOW! Women comprise 21.4 percent of the Federal Parliament of Australia, nearly double the international average of 11.7%.

WOW! 30.68% of Commonwealth's Board positions are currently filled by women.

Private Sector

WOW! Women currently comprise approximately one-third of small business owners and operators in Australia and their numbers are increasing faster than the corresponding rate for men.

WOW! 34% of Australian companies have at least one woman on their boards compared to 71% in the US or 7.6% of board members vs. 11.1% in the U.S. according to Korn/Ferry International.

WOW! Example of organization: **Australian Business Women's Network**. www.abn.org.ua/pmemform.htm.

153

CANADA

WOW! **The Canadian Government** is serious and aggressive about women's leadership. In the international sphere, it is committed to assisting small and medium-sized enterprises, particularly those owned by women, to develop more trading links, particularly with its neighbor, the United States.

Canada and the U.S. enjoy the WORLD'S largest trading relationship with more than $1 billion in goods and services moving across the border each and every day. This trading relationship was further enhanced when the first-ever Canadian businesswomen trade mission took place in November 1997. 120 businesswomen from across Canada traveled to Washington,DC, for three days of business meetings and networking. It was during that mission that Canada's Minister for International Trade, the Honorable Sergio Marchi, made two major announcements:

> **The formation of a Trade Research Coalition (TRC)** to learn more about Canadian women business owners and their international trading activities. The results of the TRC's ground-breaking work are to be announced in a cross-Canada broadcast on March 8, 1999, International Women's Day.

> **The first Canada-USA Businesswomen's Trade Summit**, May 17-21, 1999, in Toronto. This unique Summit brings together 300 women business owners (150 from each country) for three intense days of policy discussions, business matchmaking and networking. The Summit is being co-chaired by Canadian International Trade Minister Sergio Marchi, U.S. Commerce Secretary Bill Daley, and US SBA Administrator Aida Alvarez. More information is available on the Web site at www.businesswomensummit.com.

WOW! There are more than 700,000 women-led companies in Canada.

154

WOW! FACTS

WOW! More than one-third of self employed Canadians in 1996 were women, compared to 19% in 1975. *[Source: Industry Canada]*

WOW! The growth rate of these firms is twice the national rate. The number of incorporated businesses more than doubled during the last decade when the number of men with incorporated firms increased by one-third.

WOW! In Canada, women-led firms employ 1.7 million persons, more than those of "Canadian Business" Top 100 companies combined.

WOW! Women-led firms in Canada are creating new jobs at four times the average rate.

WOW! 100 key Canadian businesswomen's organizations and entities are listed in the 1998/99 BWN Directory.

WOW! Canadian women are selling their products worldwide. The US is the dominant market with 74% of exporters making sales. This compares to 60% of exporters reporting activity in Asia and 58% in Europe.

WOW! Women exporters, according to Ruth Rayman, set aggressive growth targets, anticipating in total sales and exports by more than 50% in two years. In the same period they plan to increase their needed workforce by 33%.

155

FACTS

CHINA

WOW! There were approximately 25 women's business organization missions to China in 1998. These include Women in Packaging; American Business Women International (now the Alliance of Business Women International); and the American Business Women's Association. Each of these groups network with their Chinese counterparts.

GREECE

WOW! Greece is playing a major leadership role particularly through the Euro/American Women's Council. The Fourth Annual Global Women's Forum is being held in 1999 in Athens, Greece.

IRELAND

WOW! **Women business owners in Ireland are accessing capital to grow their businesses and relying heavily on technology** – just like their American counterparts, according to a recent survey of Irish women entrepreneurs who are members of Network Ireland, a national organization for women in business in Ireland.

WOW! The survey also found that **63% of women business owners in Ireland plan to expand their businesses** by increasing sales and employment, opening new stores or expanding their part-time businesses into full-time enterprises.

WOW! **70% of Irish women entrepreneurs experienced business growth in 1997,** according to the survey, while **85% expected additional business growth in 1998.**

156

WOW! Half of Ireland's women business owners said that access to capital is a key business concern and 77% currently have bank credit available for the business needs.

WOW! For more information about Network Ireland, visit their Web site at www.ie.ibm.com/stories/women or call 353-1-455-6628. For more statistics about women-owned businesses, visit the National Foundation for Women Business Owners' web site at www.nfbwo.org.

ITALY

WOW! Statistical data (December 1997): *[Source: "Human Development Report" of the United Nations Development Programme (UNDP).]*
- **Seats in Parliament held by women: 10%**
- **Female administrators and managers: 53%**
- **Women's share of earned income: 31%**

MEXICO

[Source: "More Business, for More Women Across More Borders ~ Mas Negocios, Para Mas Mujeres a Traves de Mas Fronteras."]

WOW! Companies owned by women are in almost all areas of activity. Educational services (37%); personal services (23%); wholesale (21%) and retail (19%).

157

WOW! Women business owners are younger than their male counterparts, (34%) are between 36 and 45 years old, (35%) under 25, (25%) between 46 to 55, and (16%) are over 55 years old.

WOW! Women come into business ownership for many reasons: independence and desire to have their own business (27%); improve their standard of living (20%); interest in particular sector (16%); continue with a family business (14%); need of income after losing job (13%); and for personal challenge (10%).

WOW! Majority of business owners are married, men are 85% and women are 55%. But within the single owners, women are 24% than men 13%. Widowed, women are 13% and men are 1%. Divorced, women are 13% and men are 3%.

WOW! The importance of women in creating and promoting new businesses is very important, 61% are the founders, 18% inherited their business, 13% purchased their business and 8% obtained it trough a gift or marriage.

WOW! Women entrepreneurs in Mexico are a very important part of micro and small businesses, 20% (with up to15 employees), 11% (with 16 to 100 employees) and 4% (with over 100 employees).

WOW! Women business owners are very important contributors to family income, totaling an average to 62%; 37% of them provide more than 75% of household income.

158

FACTS

NEW ZEALAND

WOW! New Zealand was the first country in the world to give women the vote in 1893.

WOW! 57.9% of women are in the labor force. Women make up 44.6% of the labor force.

WOW! 83.4% of women school leavers have a formal qualification compared with 78.4 for men. Women make up 55.1% of tertiary (college) enrollments.

WOW! New Zealand has a female head of Government, Prime Minister Jenny Shipley and a female leader of the Opposition, the Right Honorable Helen Clark.

ROMANIA
[Source: Romanian Embassy, Economic Section]

WOW! **On October 17th, 1995 the Department of Women's Rights' Promotion and Protection (DWRPP) was established as a department of the Ministry of Labor and Social Protection. This department is headed up by a secretary of state, and has the following major objectives:**

- To analyze women working and leaving conditions into the society, and to design solution in order to eliminate the negative aspects;
- To elaborate family policies and to pass these to the related institutions;
- To elaborate legislative bills, and to propose specific amendments;

159

- To ensure a non-discriminatory access of women on the job market, and to improve their working conditions.

RUSSIA

WOW! Russia has 861,000 registered small businesses.

WOW! The Russian official business agency notes **70% of the Russia's newly registered small business firms are run by women**.

TRADE/EXPORTS

WOW! **Women are interested in exports.** The government is recruiting more small business and women's experts.

WOW! **Every $1 billion in exports supports about 113,000 in U.S. jobs.**

WOW! **Small companies are a larger portion of export producers than they were one decade ago.** Their share has jumped from **26.4% in 1987 to 30% in 1998.**

WOW! **In 5 years (1992-1997) U.S. exports for goods and services rose 50%.** The Gross Domestic Product rose 29%. The US now accounts for 13% of the worlds exports.

160

WOW! **Trade missions** for women and small business are flourishing. Note the daily announcements such as:

> "Wanted: 25 new-to-export U.S. small business seeking business and marketing opportunities to Mexico and SBA to Lead Small Business Trade Missions to Mexico City and Guadalajara March 8-12, 1999. Administrator Aida Alvarez headed this trade mission, and missions to Argentina and Canada."

WOW! **SBA Export Assistance Centers in 110 communities** can now be reached via email   For more information contact SBA: Tanya.smith@sba.gov (202) 205-6720 or richard.ginsburg@sba.gov (202) 205-6720

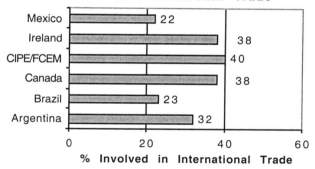

Women Business Owners are Involved in International Trade

Country	%
Mexico	22
Ireland	38
CIPE/FCEM	40
Canada	38
Brazil	23
Argentina	32

% Involved in International Trade

[Source: *International Surveys & National Foundation for Womeɪ Owners & IBM*]

161

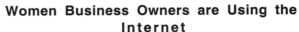 **Virtual Trade Missions (VTMs)** now allow women business owners to participate in facilitated business matching opportunities over the internet. The first Global Virtual Trade Mission included women entrepreneurs in Malaysia, Singapore and Canada. The pilot demonstrated how companies use technology to overcome the barriers of distance and travel costs. Leading multinational companies are eager to pilot VTMs. They include IBM, Lucent and Royal.

Women Business Owners are Using the Internet

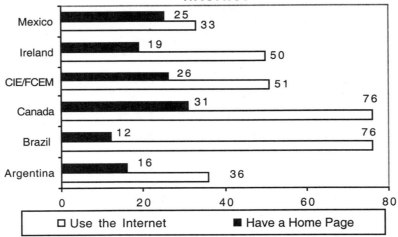

[Source: *National Foundation for Women Business Owners and IBM*]

EXPORT RESOURCES FOR BUSINESSES

Government Agencies, Examples:

- **Executive Women International,** (801) 355-2800: Executive Women International brings together over 4,000 key individuals from diverse businesses for business promotion, personal and professional development and community involvement.

- **The Trade Information Center,** run by the U.S. Department of Commerce, is the government's clearinghouse on trade information. They can be reached at (800) 872-8723 or on their Web site: www.doc.gov/tic.

- **The Export-Import Bank of the United States** provides loans, loan guarantees, and insurance. They can be reached at: (800) 565-3946, or their Web site www.exim.gov.

- **The Overseas Private Investment Corporation** offers political-risk insurance as well as loans and loan guarantees. They can be reached at: (202) 336-8799 or visit their Web site at www.opic.gov.

- **The Small Business Administration** offers information; about exporting at (800) 463-4636 and on their Web site at www.sba.gov.

- **State trade agencies**. Every state and the District of Columbia has a trade agency to help businesses that want to export.

Private Resources, Example:

- **Export Information on the Internet**. **The Unibex Global Business Center** allows users to set up a Web site and make deals on the Internet. For information, see their Web site at www.unibex.com.

163

WOW! Women's organizations are attuned to global issues. Many of them are organized for global purposes. Others are dedicated to international as well as U.S. activities.

Examples of women's organizations with global interests are:

Alliance of Business Women International (ABWI) (800) 606-2294, www.abwiworld.com. ABWI is a nonprofit organization that encourages and supports business women involved or interested in international trade opportunities. ABWI holds an annual Business Connections Trade Show, providing companies with the opportunity to meet key decision makers, exhibit their products and establish new partnerships.

Global Women's Trade Network, www.globalwomen.org. This Web site includes the virtual trademark for women entrepreneurs with their products.

Les Femmes Chef's Enterprises Mondiales (FCEM),
(301) 608-2590, www.fcem.org. The international organization for women entrepreneurs fosters the exchange on trade and entrepreneurial growth. It is comprised of members from 35 countries.

Global Fund for Women (650) 853-8305 www.globalfundforwomen.org. This grantmaking organization provides assistance for groups around the world. The Fund supports worldwide grants and has provided worldwide grants and has provided $8.5 million to 995 grassroots women's groups in 123 countries and territories.

Network of East-West Women (NEWW), (202) 265-3585. NEWW is a communications network linking over 1,500 women's advocates in

164

more than 30 countries in Europe, the Soviet Union and the United States. NEWW Online is an electronic communications network linking women's NGOs to maximize information exchange. The East-WOW! Facts information from CO: West Legal Committee examines and monitors the legal impact of the post-communist transition in women's lives.

Trade Policy Forum, (703) 971-3886. Provides an opportunity for senior women working in international trade policy to have off-the-record informal discussions on trade issues and public policy.

Women Connect Asia, (650) 654-4489. Strives to form an informational link between business women in America with interests in Asia, as well as to unite business women in Asia to create stronger bonds and contacts.

Women in International Security (WIS), (301) 405-7612. Is dedicated to enhancing opportunities for women professionals in both foreign and defense policy. WIIS serves as a clearinghouse for information for and about women in foreign and defense policy and maintains a network with Russian women researchers working on international issues.

Women in World Trade Boston, (617) 734-1408, www.capecod.net/wwt-boston.com. Women in World Trade, Boston, has become a recognized leader in the international business community and plays an important role in promoting the global network in Boston. WWT is affiliated with the Women in International Trade, with whom its shares its mission to enhance the status and interest of women in the field of international business.

Women's World Banking (WWB), (212) 768-8513. WWB is a global non-profit financial institution established to advance and promote the full economic participation of women. WWB has served over 500,000

165

clients and made 200,000 loans of small amounts to help women form micro-businesses. They are affiliated in 50 countries.

Women's Foreign Policy Group (WFPG), (202) 884-8597,www.wfpg.org.. A nonprofit, educational organization dedicated to a global engagement and the promotion of the leadership of women in international affairs professions. Mentoring programs sponsored for students offer opportunities to interact with professionals from the wide range of international affairs practices.

Alliance of American and Russian Women (AARW), (212) 730-5082. A nonprofit organization dedicated to assisting Russian women in developing and managing micro-enterprises. The primary goal of the organization is for American business women to mentor Russian women in the areas of business enterprise and the components of joint ventures.

Global Fund for Women, (650) 853-8305. A grant making organization that provides flexible and timely financial assistance to women's groups around the world. The Fund has given nearly $8.5 million to 995 grassroots women's groups in 123 countries and territories. The Fund engages in grant making, philanthropic education, fundraising, information events and talks, and international conferences.

Global Woman/Forum, (202) 775-7234. Global Woman is a program of the Forum for Intercultural Communication (Forum), a nonprofit research and education organization to address the challenges of a rapidly changing and increasingly interdependent world, by promoting economic development and local-global partnerships.

International Women's Media Foundation (IWMF), (202) 496-1992. IWMF is the only international organization of women journalists that transcends both national boundaries and professional categories. Its mission is to strengthen the role of women in the media worldwide. IWMF grants the "Courage in Journalism Awards" to women who have demonstrated extraordinary bravery and determination in bringing the news to the people.

Organization of Women in International Trade (OWIT),
(312) 641-1466. Enhances the status and interests of women in the field of international trade through the establishment of a worldwide network of international business contacts. OWIT presents the Women of the Year and Member of the Year awards at its annual conference in October.

UN Development Fund for Women (UNIFEM), (212) 906-6400. The United Nations Development Fund for Women provides direct support for women's projects and promotes the inclusion of women in the decision-making process of mainstream development programs.

UN Commission on the Status of Women (CSW), (212)-963-1234. The Commission on the Status of Women was established as a functional commission of the Economic and Social Council to prepare recommendations and reports to the Council on promoting women's rights in political, economic, civil, social and educational fields.

WOW! FACTS™

CHAPTER 14: JOBS AND CAREERS

WOW! 16% of today's workers rate their chance for advancement on the job as excellent; while 23% rate it as good; and 61% as poor.

WOW! A recent article by The Society of Human Resource Management (SHRM), cited that **20% of all working temporaries are professionals,** particularly within accounting and technology. **35% of all working women are employed as clerical workers (24.2%),** retail salespeople (7.6%), waitresses and hairdressers (2.9%).

WOW! Women make up 22% of the science and engineering labor force as a whole, and were 20% of all doctoral scientists and engineers in the United States in 1993 compared to 19% in 1991. This number continues to grow at approximately the same annual rate.

WOW! Wage increases for 1999 are expected to be moderate while 1998 increases averaged 3.5% according to the U.S. Department of Labor.

WOW! 82% of corporate CEOs claim the primary reason for women being held back from advancement to senior positions is lack of significant general management or line experience.

WOW! Demand for technology executives is up more than 32% in one year. The technology sector represents significant opportunities given its expansion due in part to the impact of the internet on communications

169

and commerce. Korn/Ferry's Advanced Technology Executive Demand Index reports that the overall executive demand in the technology sector is up 32% over 1997, and making great opening for women and minorities.

WOW! **The American worker spends an average of 44 hours per week** (paid and unpaid) – 6 hours more than they are scheduled to work.

WOW! **Women's work hours have increased from 39 to 44 hours** (or 5 hours) **per week;** while men have increased from 47.1 to 49.9 hours (or 2.8 hours) from 1977 to 1997.

WOW! **American companies invest $30 billion annually for training programs.**

WOW! **Computerized reference systems at libraries** can give you access to journals, magazines, and newspapers with pertinent articles relating to top professions and salaries earned.

Examples include:

The American Almanac of Jobs and Salaries by John W. Wright and Edward J. Dwyer (Avon Books) for industry, government, entertainment and sports salaries.

Professional Careers Source Book by Kathleen Savage and Charity Dorgan, Eds. (Gale Research Inc.) includes salary ranges for 111 careers requiring college degrees or specialized education.

American Salaries and Wages Survey by Arsen Darnay (Gale Research

170

ACTS

Inc.) contains salary information from more than 300 government, business, and news sources.

The 1992 Geographic Reference Report, published annually by the Economic Research Institute, outlines the annual median salaries for over 80 occupations in each of 280 cities in the U.S. and Canada. Good for relocating to another city, it includes cost of living data.

RESOURCES THROUGH THE GOVERNMENT

U.S. General Services Administration – Office of Enterprise Development (OED).
202-501-1021; www.gsa.gov/oed
OED conducts monthly seminars on government contracting in Washington, D.C., and at its 12 regional offices for women and minority business owners.

U.S. Department of Commerce – Office of Small and Disadvantaged Business Utilization (OSDBU).
202-482-1472; www.doc.gov/osdbu
OSDBU maintains a database on its Web site of the U.S. Department of Commerce contracting opportunities; it can be searched by SIC code.

Commerce Business Daily and Net
http://cdbnet.access.gpo.gov
A free online listing of government contracting opportunities paying at least $25,000. The print version of *Commerce Business Daily* is available for $275 a year from the U.S. Government Printing Office 888-293-6498 and can be found at many libraries.

171

CAREER SITES ON THE INTERNET

America's Job Bank (AJB)
http://it.jobsearch.org
AJB is the largest and most frequently visited job bank in cyberspace. AJB lists thousands of high-tech jobs, and many prominent high-tech companies use the Job Bank to recruit workers. AJB's new Web site is at.

America's Talent Bank
http://atb.mesc.state.ms.us
America's Talent Bank offers a national database of electronic resumes that helps employers identify good candidates for their job openings. Many high-tech workers market their skills through the Talent Bank. Thousands more will post their resumes each month as the base of high-tech jobs in America's Talent Bank grows.

America's Career InfoNet
http://www.acinet.org/acinet
America's Career InfoNet offers valuable information about the employment outlook, industry trends, training requirements, and salary structure for a company's career fields.

CareerBabe
http://www.careerbabe.com/
CareerBabe is an online job search resource for women. It aims to provide up-to-date insightful advice on the hottest career opportunities in today's job and employment markets and the most useful career information and Internet career sites, resources and resume matching services.

Digital Women
www.digital-women.com
Digital Women was created to provide a place where any woman could come to find resources to help them succeed at home and in the workplace.

172

The main goal of this Web site is to provide the tools necessary for women to succeed in business.

iVillage.com - The Women's Network
http://www.ivillage.com
iVillage humanizes cyberspace and provides a relevant and indispensable online experience for adult women. They aim to bring diverse people to their communities and facilitate the active exchange of information, advice and support on the subjects in life that matter the most: parenting, work, and health. By participating in their communities, people learn from experts and from each other, empower themselves to solve problems, and inspire others to handle everyday issues better.

Online Women's Business Center
www.onlinewbc.org
Interactive business skills training on the worldwide web. This Web site is dedicated to helping enterprising women realize their goals and aspirations for personal and professional development. The #1 goal is to provide women with the information and expertise needed to plan their business.

Job Options
www.joboptions.com The next generation in employment sites. Job Options features a searchable employer database with information on thousands of companies that are hiring, as well as a resume posting option.

Women Entrepreneurs Online Network (WEON)
www.weon.com WEON is an organization which introduces women in business with a method for exchanging ideas it promotes mentorship and networking among WEON members. It covers such topics as: building referrals, lead generation, and business opportunities.

Women's Wire
www.womenswire.com Women's Wire offers inside information on career solutions, work/life balance and management tracks. It also offers business

173

tools such as job interview kits, business plans, career quizzes and job listings.

Monster.com
www.monster.com 5 million job seekers visit Monster.com job listings each month, according to "The Industry Standard."

Hotjobs.com
Hotjobs.com is another "hot" career site. It claims more than 1 million visitors each month.

Futurestep
Futurestep haD approximately 200,000 job candidate profiles in its database as of February 1999.

Heidrick & Struggles
Heidrick & Struggles is launching its own Internet service in April 1999 for job candidates interested in high-level information technology jobs.

LAI Worldwide
LAI Worldwide has announced its planned Internet-based recruitment unit aimed at midlevel jobs.

JobWeb
JobWeb.org by the National Association of Colleges and Employers has information on internships and careers.

Vault Reports
Vault Reports has information on companies and internships on its Web site at www.vaultreports.com.

Wall Street Journal Careers
The Wall Street Journal' s Web site has general information on job searches at www.careers.wsj.com.

BEST JOBS FOR THE 21ST CENTURY

Job	Earnings	Job Openings	% of Growth
Systems Analyst	$48,360	87,318	103%
Computer Engineer	$54,912	34,884	109%
Engineering, Math and Natural Sciences Managers	$65,686	37,494	45%
Securities and Financial Services Sales	$59,634	40,568	38%
Marketing, Advertising and PR	$53,602	54,600	29%
Computer Scientists	$48,630	26,732	118%
Services Managers	$48,339	171,229	21%
Physical Therapists	$52,811	19,122	71%
Special Education Teachers	$37,104	49,029	59%
General Managers and Top Executives	$58,344	288,825	15%
Computer Programmers	$48,360	58,990	23%
Management Support Workers	$35,339	154,129	26%
Registered Nurses	$40,310	165,362	21%
Lawyers	$70,117	45,929	19%
Secondary School Teachers	$36,784	168,392	22%
Electrical and Electronics Engineers	$53,227	19,098	29%
Physicians	$96,637	29,681	21%
Financial Managers	$54,392	74,297	18%
Social Workers	$31,221	75,554	32%
College and University Faculty	$44,800	126,584	19%

[Source: BestWorks Inc, Indianapolis, IN]

WOW! Jobs employing a high percentage of women are growing much faster than lists for men.

WOW! Average job growth for the top 20 jobs for women in 59% while it is less than half that for men – 28%.

WOW! Occupations with the highest percent of men average 160,388 while women are nearly 100% more: 313,218.

WOW! Best paying jobs employing 70% or more women:

Job	% Women	Avg Annual Earnings
Pharmacists	86%	$55,328
Physical Therapists	74%	$52,811
Occupational Therapists	74%	$46,779
Speech Language Pathologists	74%	$42,702
Dental Hygienists	82%	$42,432
Insurance Claims Examiners	75%	$41,142
Physician Assistants	86%	$40,414
Registered Nurses	94%	$40,310
Cost Estimators	87%	$39,894
Nuclear Medicine Technologists	74%	$38,605
Insurance Adjusters, Investigators	75%	$38,230
Special Education	84%	$37,104
Flight Attendants	82%	$36,442
Elementary School Teachers	86%	$35,280
Cardiology Technologists	82%	$33,696
Respiratory Therapists	74%	$32,781

© Business Women's Network, Washington, DC 20036
(800) 48-WOMEN
http://www.bwni.com

FACTS

WOW! **Skills and Experience Employers Want In Their Employees:**
(Top Score is 5.00)

• Interpersonal skills	4.67
• Teamwork skills	4.65
• Analytical skill	4.56
• Oral communication skills	4.53
• Flexibility	4.52
• Computer skills	4.32
• Written communication skills	4.12
• Leadership skills	4.08
• Work experience	4.05
• Internship experience	3.77

WOW! **Top Ten Personal Characteristics**
Employers Seek in Job Candidates:

- Honesty/Integrity
- Motivation/Initiative
- Communication Skills
- Self-Confidence
- Flexibility
- Interpersonal Skills
- Strong Work Ethic
- Teamwork Skills
- Leadership Skills
- Enthusiasm

[Source: National Association of Colleges and Employers]

177

FACTS

WOW! Hot Job Tracks, according to *U.S. News & World Report*, October 26, 1998:

- Environmental accountant
- Web specialist
- Musician
- Nanny
- Technical writer
- Construction project manager
- Information technology consultant
- Speech pathologist
- Communications engineer
- Banking relationship manager
- Physical therapist
- Catering director
- Executive recruiter
- Networking architect
- Real estate attorney
- Primary-care physician

WOW! 20 Hot Careers For Women Highlighted by *Working Woman Magazine*, February 1999:

GENERAL MANAGER
Today most companies are expanding and hiring middle managers who can strategize, incorporate technology, and develop strategic partnerships with outsourcers.

ADOPTION ADVOCATE
Adoptive parents often need extensive resources in helping them deal with financial issues, administrative hearings and the paperwork

associated with adopting children. Adoption advocates are often social workers, but organizations such as the North American Council on Adoptable Children are working to create on-the-job training.

STAFFING SERVICE COORDINATOR
In the past decade, the ranks of temporary, contingency, and project workers have grown by 163% into a veritable army.

EXECUTIVE RECRUITER
The current job market has boomed for the executive-recruiting business. The number of placements made by executive search consultants rose by 18% in 1997.

CORPORATE INTELLIGENCE
Utilizing newspaper articles, competitor's sales material and credit reports, the corporate intelligence officer analyzes the company's industry competitor and predicts future trends.

KNOWLEDGE MANAGER
Making useful information accessible to the employees of an organization is the job of the knowledge manager. Knowledge managers access books, magazines, and the Internet and organize the gathered information into databases.

COLLECTIONS MANAGER
Database skills and administrative abilities are not the only requirements for collections managers as they must also infuse enthusiasm to collectors dealing with angry consumers.

BUSINESS PROCESS CONSULTANT
The goal of this position is to find the problem, whether it is inefficient use of machines, manufacturing glitches, or unhappy corporate environments, diagnose it and then help solve the situation.

179

FACTS

BUSINESS TO BUSINESS SERVICE SALES
By studying customers' needs, salespeople anticipate how their products and their customers' goals coincide. Sensitivity to the customers' potential problems and an in-depth knowledge of the customer is key for successful salespeople.

DATABASE INTEGRATOR
Because computers house a great deal of the information for many corporations, it is the database integrator's responsibility to provide the technical link between the older and latest computers.

E-COMMERCE PROJECT MANAGER
The goal of this position is to first create a web page which convinces the customer that the products the company is selling are what they need and second, to ensure that the warehouses and delivery operations are coordinated for efficiency for the e-commerce. Both marketing and administrative skills are essential.

CORPORATE CONCIERGE
This is the professional errand position with duties including buying gifts, ordering tickets and getting flowers for the employees of the organization. Candidates should be enthusiastic and precision-oriented.

SOFTWARE INTERFACE DESIGNER
Making software programs easy to use for the customers without them having to rely on the manual is the job of the software interface designer. The designer works with engineers to make the computer user's experience as painless as possible.

CUSTOMER SERVICE MANAGER
Communication with the customer is key to this position, as customer service managers must follow-up and troubleshoot product and service problems to retain customer loyalty. In order to do this, the managers customize products and ascertain better ways to serve the customer.

WOW!
FACTS

INVESTOR RELATIONS SPECIALIST
The goal of the investor relations specialist is to motivate executives such as shareholders and brokers to invest in the company.

SPECIAL EVENTS PLANNER
Organizational skills are a must for this job that requires that corporate get-togethers are immaculate, from the food to the environment. These special events can include private board of director dinners to large-scale conventions.

TELECOMMUTING MANAGER
The teleconferencing, email and the use of Internet turned an estimated 8% of the work force into telecommuters. Corporations and governments are increasingly using telecommuting for their efficiency.

ACCESSIBILITY CONSULTANT
Corporate, commercial and public facilities must now be designed or redesigned to accommodate people with disabilities. This has resulted in a new career that combines architecture, design, and rehabilitative services.

PATIENT REPRESENTATIVE
With an increasing complicated health care system, the HMO's hospitals, nursing homes, and clinics are hiring patient representatives, or healthcare advocates.

[Note: For salary and contact information on these careers see *Working Woman Magazine*; February 1999.]

FACTS

WOW! A University of Michigan study cites internships as most important to getting a job.

WOW! Women entrepreneurs are recruiting interns through a variety of programs.

WOW! Internships for women are often vital to careers. BWN offers these examples:

American Association of University Women (AAUW)
Contact: Internship Coordinator at (202) 785-7700.

Business Women's Network (BWN)
3–to-4 month internships.
Contact: Internship Coordinator at (800)-48-WOMEN, or by fax at (202) 833-1808.

CyberGirl
4–to-6 month internships.
Contact: maureen@cgim.com.

Emily's List
4-month internships offered at this leading women's political organization.
Contact: Internship Coordinator at (202) 326-1400.

Essence Magazine
6-week summer internships at pre-eminent magazine for African American women.
Contact: Internship Coordinator at (212) 642-0700

Feminist Majority
2-month internships are offered at this women's rights organization based in Los Angeles, CA and Arlington, VA.
Contact: Los Angeles: (213) 651-0495; Arlington, VA: (703) 522-2214.

Focus on Women
12–to-17 week internships are offered at the Henry Ford Community College in Dearborn, MI.
Contact: Focus on Women
Henry Ford Community College
5101 Evergreen Road
Dearborn, MI 48128
Telephone: (313) 845-9629, Fax: (313) 845-9852, E-mail: grace@mail.henryford.cc.mi.us

MacDonald Communications
12-week internships.
Contact: Internship Coordinator at (212) 446-6100.

Ms. Magazine
15–to-20 week internships are offered at this prominent women's issues magazine.
Contact: 212-445-6162.

My Sister's Place
Public service internships are arranged at the violence-against-women center shelter.
Contact: Volunteer Coordinator at (202) 529-5261, or by fax at (202) 529-5984.

FACTS

National Association of Female Executives (NAFE)
10–to-12 week internships are offered at this, the largest organization of business women in the U.S.
Contact: (212) 425-6100.

National Women's Health Network
12-week internships are offered   at   this health care public policy organization.
Contact: Internship Coordinator at (202) 347-1140 or by fax at
(202) 347-1168.

Seventeen Magazine
6-week internships in New York City.
Contact: Internship Coordinator at (212) 407-9700.

UN Development Fund for Women (UNIFEM)
Contact: Internship Coordinator at (212) 906-6543.

The Washington Center for Internships and Academic Seminars
10–to-15 week internships in Washington, DC   are arranged through the Washington Center's Women's Leadership Program.
Contact: (800) 486-8921 or www.twc.edu.

Women Express
12-week public services internships in Boston, MA at publisher of *Teen Voices*.
Contact: Internship Coordinator at (617) 426-5505.

Women Make Movies (WMM)
12-week internships in New York, NY.
Contact: Internship Coordinator at (212) 925-0606 or by fax at
(212) 925-2052.

184

FACTS

Women's Institute for Freedom
Contact: (202) 966-7783 or by E-mail wifonline@igc.apc.org.

Women's International League for Peace and Freedom
12-week internships at human rights organization based in Philadelphia, PA; New York, NY; and Geneva, Switzerland.
Contact: Internship Coordinator at (215) 763-7100 or by E-mail at wilpfnatl@igc.org.

Women's Legal Defense Fund
12–to-16 week internships are offered at this women's issues and public policy organization.
Contact: Internship Coordinator at (202) 986-2600 or by fax at (202) 986-2539.

Women's Project & Productions (WPP)
Off-Broadway theater organization that develops the works of women playwrights and directors.
Contact: Internship Coordinator at (212) 765-1706 or fax (212) 765-2024.

Women's Sports & Fitness Magazine
16-to-18 week internships are offered in Boulder, CO.
Contact: (303) 444-5111 or fax: (303) 444-3313.

Women's Sports Foundation
3–to-6 month internships are offered on Long, Island, NY.
Contact: Internship Coordinator at (516) 542-4700 or (800) 227-3988.

185

JOB SEARCH & CAREER GUIDANCE

National Best Sellers:

- **What Color is Your Parachute?** (1999 Edition), by Richard Bolles (Ten Speed Press, Berkley, California.)
- **Knock 'Em Dead 1999**, by Martin Yate (Adams Publishing.)
- **Cover Letters That Knock 'Em Dead**, by Martin Yate (Adams Publishing.)
- **Cool Careers for Dummies**, by Marti Nemko, Paul Edwards & Sarah Edwards (IDG Publishing.)
- **Resumes that Knock 'Em Dead**, by Martin Yate (Adams Publishing.)
- **Do What You Are**, by Barbara and Paul Tieger (Little, Brown & Co.)
- **Resumes for Dummies**, by Joyce Lain Kennedy (IDG Books.)
- **Discover What You Are Best At**, Linda Gale (Simon & Schuster.)
- **101 Great Answers to the Toughest Interview Questions**, by Ronald Fry (Career Press.)
- **Job Interviews for Dummies**, by Joyce Lain Kennedy (IDG Books.)

[Source: Barnes & Noble Inc. survey of job-search and career-guidance book sales in Barnes & Noble, B. Dalton Bookseller, Bookstop, Bookstar, Doubleday and Scribners bookstores nationwide conducted for the National Business Employment Weekly.]

Calendar of Events

Career Events – Hundreds of Events are occurring in every city every week. We list only 1/2 of 1% of the examples we found in one week's time. Examples from *National Employment Weekly*:

- Sacramento Professional Network, Experience Unlimited, California Employment Development Department, 5007 Broadway, Sacramento, CA, 95820. (916) 227-0330, Fax: (916) 227-0382.

- Turning Point Career Center, YWCA, 2600 Bancroft Way, Berkeley, CA, 94704, (510) 848-6370.
- CareerPoint, 850 High St., Holyoke, MA, 01040, (413) 532-4900.

- Women's Opportunities Center, University of California, Irvine, and P.O. Box 6050, Irvine, CA, 92616, (949) 824-7128.

- San Francisco Chamber of Commerce, 465 California St. (9th Floor), San Francisco, CA, 94104, (415) 392-4520.

- Employment Opportunity & Training Center of Northeastern Pennsylvania, Kane Building, Suite 3D, 116 North Washington, Avenue, Scranton, PA., 18503, (717) 348-6484.

- Business & Professional Exchange, P.O. Box 50372, Indianapolis, IN, 46250, (317) 252-9947 (North Chapter) or (317) 882-1012 (South Chapter).

- Career/HiTech Connection, 400 W. Campbell Rd., Richardson, TX, 75080, (972) 238-8737, Fax: (972) 238-8214.

- Experience Unlimited, Professionals Plus Networking Group, 1420 West Avenue I, Lancaster, CA., 93534, (805) 726-4149, Contact: Bennie R. Thornton.

WOW! FACTS™

CHAPTER 15: EDUCATION

HIGH SCHOOL AND COLLEGE

WOW! Although boys slightly outnumber girls in the 15-19 age group, **more girls graduate from high school.** In 1996, **51% of high school graduates were girls.** *[Source: U.S. News and World Report]*

WOW! **70% of female high school graduates are currently** enrolled in college, **compared to only 18% in 1973. Only 60.1% of male high school graduates enroll in college.**

WOW! In 1994, 27% of females finished four years of college compared to 18% in 1971.

WOW! Women earned 54% of all BA degrees awarded in the United States in 1997. By 2007, women will earn 58% of all BA degrees.

WOW! Women earn more than **half of all bachelor's degrees in psychology and social sciences,** but **only one-third of the bachelor degrees in mathematics and physical sciences. 16% of bachelor degrees in engineering are earned by women.**

WOW! The U.S. Department of Education projects that **by 2008 women will outnumber men in undergraduate and graduate programs by 9.2 to 6.9 million.**

189

GRADUATE SCHOOL

WOW! Between 1994 and 1995, women earned **23% more master's degrees than men.**

WOW! **Women earned 52% of all masters degrees and 40% of all doctoral degrees between 1994 and 1995.**

WOW! In 1995, 37% of all students in business school were women.

WOW! **Women were 36% of the graduate students enrolled in science and engineering in 1993, and were 30% of science and engineering doctorate recipients that year.** These numbers are growing rapidly as more and more women move into the field of technology.

WOW! In 1995, 39% of all medical students were women compared to 1% in 1972.

WOW! In 1996, 44% of all law students were women, compared to only 7% in 1971.

190

Business Schools are becoming far more important to women as we move up the corporate ladder and realize for a job in the corporate world in particular or to learn the skills of an entrepreneur, this training is important. **The Top 10 Business Schools for Women** from *Working Woman Magazine*, October 1998:

- **Columbia University Graduate School of Business**
  New York, NY, (212) 854-1961
- **University of Michigan Business School**
  Ann Arbor, MI; (734) 763-5796
- **University of California at Berkeley School of Business** Berkeley, CA; (510) 642-1405
- **Northwestern University Graduate School of Management**
  Evanston, IL; (847) 491-3300
- **The University of Virginia, Darden Graduate School of Business Administration**
  Charlottesville, VA; (804) 924-7281
- **Stanford University Graduate School of Business**
  Stanford, CA (650) 723-2766
- **Duke University, The Fuqua School of Business**
  Durham, NC; (919) 660-7705
- **University of North Carolina, The Kenan-Flagler Business School** Chapel Hill, NC; (919) 962-8301
- **Ohio State University, The Fisher College of Business** Columbus, OH; (614) 292-8531
- **The University of Pennsylvania, Wharton School Graduate Division** Philadelphia, PA; (215) 898-6183

EDUCATION LEADERSHIP

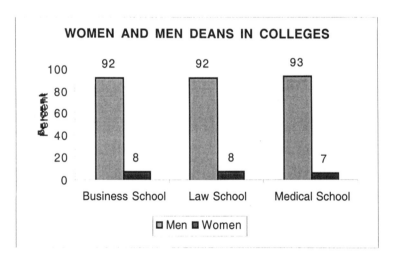

WOW! Women hold only a small percentage of positions as college presidents and deans; **500 women are presidents of colleges and universities, or 16%** of such positions in accredited undergraduate schools. (This is an increase from 148 women in 1977.) **Nine women are deans of medical schools, or 7%.**

WOW! University-based Policy Research Centers (28) have developed **alliances for scholarships, advocacy, policy and action for women and girls.**

WOMEN AND MEN DEANS IN COLLEGES

192

FACTS

WOMEN'S RIGHTS AND EDUCATION

WOW! It was 1848 when 300 women met in **Seneca Falls, NY** to proclaim the **Women's Bill of Rights**. **Title IX** was passed by Congress on June 23, 1972. This prohibited discrimination against students and employees in educational institutions receiving federal funds. Title IX increased opportunities for women and girls in athletics, access to higher education, career education and employment. It improved learning environments such as science for girls and provided fairness of standardized testing and eliminated sexual harassment and pregnancy discrimination.

WOW! Women have made great gains, with credit attributable to Title IX. Educational opportunities for girls have increased substantially since 1972 (*National Business Women*). Progress, according to the Education Department's Report: **Title IX: 25 Years of Progress is evident**:

- **College Enrollment**: 63% of female high school graduates are enrolled in college compared to 18% in 1973.

- **College Degrees**: 27% finished four years of college in 1994 vs. 18% 23 years earlier, in 1971.

- **Professional Degrees**:

    Law – Women earned **43%** of law degrees in 1994, 44% in 1996, **48%** in 1998, compared to only 7% in 1971.
    Medical – Women earned **38%** medical degrees in 1994, 39% in 1995, and **42%** compared to nine percent in 1972.
    Dental – Women earned **38%** of dental degrees in 1994 compared with only **1%** in 1972.

193

- **Graduate Ph.D.s**: Women earned 44% of all doctoral degrees in 1997, compared to 25% in 1977.

- **Intercollegiate Athletics**: Women participate increasingly: 100,000 in 1998, compared to 25,000 in 1971. **High School Athletics**: Today 2.4 million you women participate in high school athletics compared to 300,000 in 1971. That's 39% in 1996 vs. 7.5% in 1971.

WOMEN'S COLLEGES

WOW! *1998-99 BWN Directory* includes profiles of 160 college and university women's organizations. Among these college and university organizations, 150 have Web sites. *The Directory* includes Web site profiles of 30 women's colleges and over 90 university women's resource centers.

WOW! Women's colleges continue to provide women with valuable learning environments, some 40 of these colleges now can be seen on the Internet. Another 150 women's colleges, universities, and student organizations have made homes on the Internet. Nearly 145 women's Web sites provide some type of education to their members by means of special programs. College and university Web sites traditionally were little more than online calendars and contact pages. However, many have grown in sophistication to rival the Web sites of other organizations.

WOW! **Graduates of women's colleges outperform women graduates of coeducational institutions:**

- Graduates of women's colleges are seven times more likely to pursue careers in traditionally male-dominated, higher paying fields such as law, medicine, business management and computer science.

194

FACTS

- More than one third of the women board members of Fortune 1000 companies are women's college graduates

- The median salary for women's college graduates exceeds the national average for women with college degrees.

- More than 80% of women's college graduates pursue graduate studies and more than 50% earn advanced degrees. They are more than twice as likely to earn doctorates, particularly in the natural sciences, and to enter medical school.

195

CHAPTER 16: YOUNGER WOMEN

WOW! Members of the Generation X workforce (18–to–32 years of age in 1997) are **better educated and more racially and ethnically aware** than their contemporaries 20 years ago.

WOW! Contrary to the media's image of Generation X-ers, **young workers today work substantially longer hours and find their jobs more demanding than those of the same age group 20 years ago.**

WOW! **Youth are major purchasers.** Take even the malls. According to the International Council of Shopping Centers, those from age 14 to 24 comprise 26% of all mall shopping.

WOW! **Young women are likely to own a computer.** According to Roper Starch Worldwide, 39% of those 18-29 now own a home PC compared to 25% in 1993.

WOW! There are numerous organizations who support girls and/or **young women. The following examples are meant to be illustrative, not comprehensive:**

Youth Organization Examples:

Girls Incorporated Headquarters (GIH), 212-689-3700
Girls Incorporated is a national nonprofit organization noted for developing and implementing informal educational programs that compensate for

197

gender inequities and tackle tough societal issues facing today's girls and young women.

An Income of Her Own, Inc., (805) 646-1215.

An Income of Her Own supports the economic empowerment of the next generation through mentor training for parents, teachers and youth organizations. They also present the "Annual National Business Plan Awards for Teen Women."

National Association of Women in Construction, (817) 877-5551.

NAWIC sponsors "Career Days" to promote the construction industry as a viable choice to junior and high school students. The "NAWIC Block Kids" program is a national building competition that promotes construction careers to children in grades one through six. NAWIC Founders' Scholarship Foundation awards grants each year to college students pursuing construction related degrees.

Women of Color Resource Center (WCRC), (510)-848-9272.

"Girls are the Issue" is a high school curriculum project inspired by the Beijing Platform for Action. The objectives are to make students aware of the critical areas of concern addressed in the Platform for Action, to increase students' awareness of the conditions facing young women and girls in other parts of the world.

The Women of Color Resource Centers helps to familiarize students with the kinds of activities women have undertaken to address these conditions, and to facilitate exchanges between school and community on the critical areas of concern.

198

FACTS

Dare To Dream Foundation, (561) 883-9918.
Dare to Dream Foundation strives to give every girl in America a dream. Girls are empowered to facilitate a positive outlook on their futures which will affect their personal growth. In order to achieve its mission, the Dare to Dream Foundation also provides middle schools with inspirational videos of positive women role models and live mentors.

Two current projects are the development of an elementary school program, as well as a female "encarta," which would eventually and ideally bring the aspirations of young women to at least the level of young men's. Dare to Dream is reaching out through more than 100,000 high schools.

AAUW Educational Foundation (202) 728-7602
AAUW supports young women through its Fellowships. For example, American Fellowships support women doctoral candidates completing dissertations or scholars seeking funds for post-doctoral research leave.

Institute for Women in Trades, Technology and Science
(202) 686-7275
There are many programs sponsored by the Institute.
The Institute sponsors a "School-To-Work program: Preparing Young Women for Non-Traditional Jobs." There are other programs, one called "School-To-Work program: Preparing Young Women for Non-Traditional Careers."

Ms. Foundation for Women and the "Take Our Daughters to Work Program (212) 742-2300.
This program has become one of the most popular as it has grown nationwide. On the fourth Thursday in April each year, the program is reaching out to more than one million girls now.

199

WOW! FACTS

WOW! The June 1998 issue of *Working Woman Magazine* featured a list of **20 successful women under age 30**, representing a new generation of leaders. That list is presented below. The talented women featured on the list embody the ideals of confidence and perseverance that have knocked down potential career barriers. They all regard a myriad of fields with entirely fresh perspectives. These leaders of the future represent a creative versatility that has ensured them success.

YOUTH EXAMPLES:

Christy Haubegger, 29, Founder and Publisher, Latina Magazine, New York, NY

Rebecca Culberson, 29, Vice President and Assistant to the Chairman, Fannie Mae Organization, Washington, DC

Ani diFranco, 26, Founder and President, Righteous Babe Records, Buffalo, NY

Tina Thornton, 26, Coordinating Producer, ESPN, Connecticut.

Mary Rodas, 22, Vice President, Marketing, Catco, New York

Lisa Guerra, 29, Design Engineer, Rockwell Semiconductor Systems, CA

Terri Chi, 25, Senior Asia Segment Manager, Bank of America, San Francisco, CA

Mellody Hobson, 28, Senior Vice President, Ariel Capital Management & Mutual Funds, Chicago, IL

Heather Lamm, 27, Chair, Third Millennium, New York

Christy Jones, 28, President, pcOrder.com, Texas

Lela Headd, 28, Account Executive, Deutsch, Chicago, IL.

Erica Hamilton, 28, Banking Officer, Franchise Systems Finance, Chase Bank of Texas, Houston, TX

Eleanor Manson Keare, 27, Manager, McKinsey & Co., Dallas, TX

Julie Su, 29, Staff Attorney, Asian Pacific American Legal Center, Los Angeles, CA

Susan Athey, 27, Assistant Professor of Economics, Massachusetts Institute of Technology, Cambridge, MA

Rebecca Zucker, 29, Manager, Strategic Planning, Disney Consumer Products, FL

Liz Davidson, 26, Founder and CEO, Davidson Andrade, San Francisco, CA

Jennifer Harris, 29, Flight Director, Mars Pathfinder NASA Jet Propulsion Lab, Pasadena, CA

Aerin Lauder, 27, Director of Creative Product Development, Estee Lauder, Inc., New York

Annelise Barron, 29, Assistant. Professor of Chemical Engineering, Northwestern University, Chicago, IL

CHAPTER 17: GENDER EQUITY

WOMEN'S EARNINGS VS. MEN'S

WOW! **In 1997, women were paid only 74 cents for every dollar that men received for equal work**. Minority women have an even higher pay gap. African-American women earn 64 cents, and Hispanic-American women earn 53 cents for every dollar earned by men. About **60% of the improvement in the wage gap** during the last 15 years can be **attributed to the decline in men's real earnings**.

WOW! **350 women's organizations have joined together to celebrate Equal Pay Day** (**April 8. 1999.**) This program is designed to bring awareness of the pay gap. More than 15 states have enacted legislation making unequal pay for equal work a violation. Contact the National Committee for Pay Equity, (202) 331-7343.

WOW! **Women made less than men in every one of the more than 30 occupations surveyed by the U.S. Department of Labor. Worst Offenders**: Financial Managers; Marketing; Advertising, and Public Relations Managers; Lawyers; Designers; and Physicians.

WOW! The average **woman loses approximately $420,000 over a lifetime due to unequal pay practices.**

WOW! College educated African-American women and Hispanic-American women annually earn **$17,549 and $14,779, respectively, less**

than their white male colleagues. College educated African-American women earn less, on U. S. average, than white male high school graduates.

WOW! In the U. S. **33% of working women hold low wage jobs compared to 20% of men.**

WOW! **Worldwide, women hold only 14% of administrative and managerial jobs,** and less than 6% of senior management jobs.

WOW! **Women receive no wages for more than 66% of the work that they do.**

WOW! Conversely, **women make up three-fifths or 60% of all adults living in poverty; 13% of all women living in poverty** (1990 Census).

1). Caucasian women 9.8% in poverty
2). Asian-American women 12.8% in poverty
3). Hispanic-American women 24.3% in poverty
4). African-American women 28.9% in poverty
5). American Indian women 29.2% in poverty

WOW! Of the 14 million families maintained by women, 4.2 million had incomes below the poverty line. This is 34.6% of all families with female householders.

WOW! Women are less than half as likely to receive a pension and those who do get half as much.

© Business Women's Network, Washington, DC 20036
(800) 48-WOMEN
http://www.bwni.com

WOW! On December 18, 1979, the United Nations adopted the Convention on the Elimination of All Forms of Discrimination Against Women (CEDAW). **As of 1999, the United States Senate has not ratified this treaty.** The Convention provides a universal definition of discrimination against women so that those who would discriminate on the basis of sex can no longer claim that no clear definition exists.

WOW! **As of 1999, Congress has not yet passed** Alice Paul's Equal Rights Amendment. It would allow the 35 states which have ratified the ERA to remain counted and require the approval of only three more states for ratification of the Constitutional Amendment. (Note: remember it took women 72 years to get the right to vote.)

WOW! **The U.S. and Korea** are the only industrialized nations that have failed to sign the 1951 Equal Remuneration Convention of the International Labor Organization of the United Nations – endorsing the principle of equal pay for work of equal value.

WOW! **The Ford Foundation has awarded $1.1 million to help the new Simmons College Center for Gender and Organizations** in Boston, MA. The goal is to explore new ways of thinking about gender in the workplace which can spark innovations with a positive bottom line impact.

WOW! **The Women in Cable and Telecommunications Foundation** and Cablevision Magazine cite a 1997 study that shows approximately $7,000 salary difference between women and men. Yet a higher percentage of female survey respondents (50.5% of women vs. 31.1% of men) have undergraduate or advanced degrees. A third inequity fact, men's bonuses increased 33% vs. 9% for women over a year's period, from 1996 to 1997.

203

CHAPTER 18: DIVERSITY

DIVERSITY

WOW! In the U.S. population there are:
- 34 million African-Americans, or 12.7% of the population;
- 30.7 million Hispanic-Americans, or 11.3%, and;
- 30 million Asian-Americans, or 11%.

WOW! The Census Bureau predicts that both the African- American and Hispanic-American populations will reach 36 million by the year 2005. The Asian-American population will be about 30 million at that time.

WOW! Minorities will make up more than one-third of the U.S. population by the year 2010 – one decade from now. By the year 2050, more than half of all Americans will be "minorities".

WOW! The Hispanic-American population is projected to be the largest minority group in the U.S. by the year 2010, with some 40 million people.

WOW! The number of African-American and Hispanic-Americans in professional specialties and management has grown by almost 40% since 1994 compared with 10% for Caucasians.

WOW! Asian-American lead in entrepreneurship, and Asian business owners have higher assets than those of other minority groups.

205

BUYING POWER OF MINORITIES

WOW! Growth in the minority market is anticipated to surge. According to Hemisphere Inc., the multicultural market for products and services in the U.S. is nearing $1 trillion.

WOW! African-Americans are expected to spend more than $533 billion this year; they were spending $450 billion per year at the last calculation, and $308 billion in 1990.

WOW! Hispanic-Americans spend $380 billion per year.

WOW! African-Americans and Hispanic-American populations account for 20% or more of the total buying power in four U.S. States - New Mexico, Texas, New York and California- and in the District of Columbia.

WOW! Asian-Americans are spending close to $100 billion annually. **This is a 150% increase over the past 15 years. [Source: The University of Georgia's Selig Center for Economic Growth]**

The diversity purchasing marketing is exploding and corporations are recognizing it with billions now directed at the minority purchasers, 81% are women.

206

MINORITY WOMEN ENTREPRENEURS

WOW! 13% of all women-owned businesses in the U.S. are owned by minority women.

WOW! There are 1.1 million companies owned by minority women, employing 1.7 million people and generating over $184 billion in sales.

WOW! 37% of firms owned by minority women are owned by African-Americans.

WOW! 35% of firms owned by minority women are owned by Hispanic-Americans.

WOW! Women of Asian, American Indian or Alaskan Native heritage own 28% of all firms owned by minority women.

WOW! Between 1987 and 1996, employment in all minority women-owned firms increased by 153%, with Hispanic-American's growth being the greatest at 206%.

WOW! More than half of the firms owned by minority women (56%) are in the private sector. **19% are in retail trades and 8% are in finance, insurance and real estate.**

207

WOW! Trends show that the greatest growth in the number of firms owned by minority women has been in areas that are non-traditional. **There has been a 319% increase in construction, a 276% increase in wholesale trade, and a 253% increase in transportation, communications and public utilities.**

WOW! Women minority entrepreneurs are less likely than Caucasian women entrepreneurs to currently have bank credit. **Less than 50% of the minority women have bank credit compared to 60% of the Caucasian women business owners.**

MINORITY WOMEN IN TELEVISION AND THE MEDIA

WOW! A recent study of women in television, by Dr. Martha M. Lauzen, Professor of Communication at San Diego State University, concluded that women were underrepresented on screen and behind the scenes in the 1997-1998 top rated primetime shows. **Dr. Lauzen's study indicated that it is a myth that things are getting better for women in television. Her data included the following:**

- Overall, women comprised only 21% of directors, creators, executives, producers, writers, editors, and directors of photography;
- Not one woman director of photography was found on of any program analyzed;
- The number of women working in powerful roles declined;
- Women accounted for 39% of all characters;
- The percent of male characters in their 40's (22%) was almost double that of females of that age;
- About 81% of female characters were white, 12% were African American, 2% were Asian-American, and 1% were Hispanic-American.

208

WOW! Advertising, marketing and human resource efforts are all becoming sophisticated in their approach to a diverse marketplace and workforce.

WOW! Multicultural/minority media outlets are growing so fast they are hard to track.

MINORITY MEDIA OUTLETS

African-American	Hispanic-American	Asian-American
1,479	1,174	608

[Source: Abbott Wood Media Marketing]

WOW! **Examples of Minority Publications:**

Essence Magazine, Financial Independence Journal, Jet, Minorities and Women in Business, Latina Style, Modern, Minority Business Entrepreneur, Today's Black Woman.

Network and cable television are hot for women both for leadership opportunities and for women viewers.

WOW! **The Women in Cable & Telecommunications (WICT)** has 22 chapters and nearly 4,000 members. The positives are recognized along with the negatives, such as pay equity problems. Examples of their initiatives include two studies: "Eighteen Percent Less" -- the WICT Foundation's white paper report on salary parity between men and women working for video programmers, and: "The 15% Gap" – the Foundation's white paper report on salary parity between men and women working for multiple video distribution service (MVDS) companies—cable operators, satellite distributors.

209

WOW! **Women in Film (WIF)**, has more than 40 chapters and 12,000 members worldwide. It focuses on educational services and technology education for women in the entertainment industry. http://WIFLA@aol.com

Television and Internet are focusing on women viewers. Two prime examples are: LIFETIME Television and Oxygen Media.

WOW! **LIFETIME** was created in 1984, has grown dramatically. It was named 'Television for Women' in 1994, followed by an ambitious expansion of original programming and public service initiatives targeted to women. LIFETIME is dedicated to contemporary entertainment and information and: movies; personality profiles and interviews; information; specials; entertainment.

- LIFETIME is now available on more than 8,300 cable systems and alternative delivery systems nationwide, serving over 71 million households.
- LIFETIME is attracting record number of women viewers.
- LIFETIME currently ranks number one among women viewers, ages 18-49, outdelivering all other basic cable networks.
- LIFETIME currently ranks number one in primetime for working women, outdelivering all other basic cable networks.
- Learn about LIFETIME Television by visiting the Web site: http://wwwlifetimetv.com.

WOW! **Internet and Television:** Watch for Oxygen Media to create a media brand to reach women by combining the best qualities of the Internet and television. Gerry Laybourne pioneered the creation of branded programming for children and women as the head of Nickelodeon and Disney/ABC Cable, and was one of the highest-ranking women in the television industry.

210

Oxygen Media: Since its inception, Oxygen has acquired and overseen its online sites (Thrive, Moms Online, Electra, Oprah Online), entered into a multi-year anchor tenancy, programming and promotional partnerships.

CORPORATE DIVERSITY EFFORTS

WOW! The demand for a diversified workforce is a reality. Some **33.5% of new entrants to the workforce are either racial or ethnic minorities or women, according to Derald Wing Sue, Professor at the California State University at Haywood.**

WOW! The Center for Creative Leadership **surveyed 300 of the Fortune 1000 Companies about their diversity programs. The data they reported included the following:**

- **85% of the corporations have** policies **against racism and sexism;**
- **76% of the corporations have** grievance procedures;
- **69% report** company programs for external diversity training **and seminars;**
- **61% report** active EEO or Affirmative Action **committees or offices;**
- **53% report** corporate internship programs **supportive of diversity;**
- **50% have** internal audits, **employee attitude surveys, and other means of feedback.**

WOW! The largest study of women of color in senior corporate **management was done by Catalyst in the fall of 1998. Fifty-seven percent of the 1,700 women surveyed were satisfied with their jobs. Sixty-six percent experienced barriers to advances, such as not getting desirable assignments.**

211

WOW! Corporations rate the importance of their diversity efforts as follow:

- **83% of the corporations rate** diversity policies **as important;**

- **68% of the corporations rate** grievance procedures **as important;**

- **50% rate** top management **as being public and repeated advocates of diversity internally and externally to the corporation;**

- **50% rate** partnerships with educational institutions **as important;**

- **45% rate** job performance **rating and review as important regarding diversity;**

- **49% rate** conduct of targeting recruiting programs **for women and people of color for non-managerial positions as important;**

- **49% rate** company programs for external training **and seminars as important;**

- **47% rate** internal audits, employee attitude surveys **as important;**

- **44% rate** corporate internship programs **supportive of diversity as important;**

- **41% cite the** importance of top management being really active **for diversity;**

- **39% rate active EEO or Affirmative Action committees or offices as important.**

212

FACTS

American Express
- One of the ways that American Express seeks to serve the needs of diverse business markets is through the Diversity Business Partnership Group, which reaches out to national organizations, small businesses, and city and state governments.

BellSouth
- Affirmative Action, equal employment policies and generous charitable giving remain mainstays at corporations such as BellSouth.
- As Duane Ackerman, BellSouth's chairman and chief executive officer, says, "we work hard to serve all of our customers and support the communities in which we do business."
- 26% of the company's domestic workforce are minority employees, and more than half of BellSouth's managers are minorities or women.

Chase Manhattan Corporation
- Nearly 25,000 employees, including every member of senior management, have participated in diversity training.
- Training clearly has a bottom-line benefit, as evidenced by Chase's annual climate survey, which last year revealed that people who participated in diversity training were more positive about their overall work experience than those who had not gone through training.
- Chase Capital Partners (CCP), the company's private equity arm, is using an Internet Web site as part of its mentoring program. The Web site provides an effective tool to achieve the mentor program's goals of increased communication, networking, and relationship building.

213

FACTS

Dun & Bradstreet (D&B)
- The Minority and Women-Owned Business Development Group is just one example of Dun & Bradstreet's understanding of the need to focus on diversity as a business imperative.
- The company is also trying to increase its market share with large global customers.

Ford Motor Company
- The understanding that diversity is good for business is clear at Ford Motor Company, where diversity is driven from the top down.
- Impressive results have been achieved in areas from workforce diversity to supplier relations to dealer owner ship.
- Women represent nearly 20% of Ford's workforce, and minorities nearly 22%.
- In the area of supplier relations, Ford is the first corporation to achieve purchases of $2 billion in minority purchases, with 1997 totals reaching $2.2 billion.
- By the year 2000 Ford Motor Company intends to have 5% of its purchases made from minority suppliers.

IBM Corporation
- IBM Corporation has long been known as a diversity pioneer, having hired its first disabled employee in 1914 (the year the company was founded), its first professional woman in 1935, and its first black salesman in 1946.
- To support its workforce and gain market insights, IBM has eight executive diversity task forces, each representing a different constituency: women, African-Americans, Hispanic-Americans, Asian- Americans, Native Americans, disabled employees, gays/lesbians, and white males.

214

FACTS

PriceWaterhouseCoopers Corporation
- The recent merger of professional services powerhouses, Cooper & Lybrand and Price Waterhouse to form PriceWaterhouseCoopers PriceWaterhouseCoopers next:
- Corporation meant the blending of two cultures that highly value diversity.
- One of the first orders of business for the new organization was the formation of their Diversity Champions Group, a task force with representatives from each service line.
- PriceWaterhouseCoopers Corporation has also entered into a diversity partnership with the University of Notre Dame.

Pitney Bowes Corporation
- Within the last year Pitney Bowes, which has a history of diversity leadership, has proactively sought to build strategic relationships in several ways, including an affinity agreement with the US Hispanic Chamber of Commerce.
- Pitney Bowes has also been working in conjunction with *Black Enterprise Magazine* and the Black Chamber of Commerce.
- One of Pitney Bowes sources of information on minority- and women-owned business is Dun & Bradstreet (D&B), whose Minority and Women-Owned Business Development Group was created in 1997 to support this rapidly expanding sector.
- To encourage interchange and communication between employee of diverse backgrounds, the company has set up a chat room, which enables employees from around the world to share ideas with one another.

Sears
- Sears has made an overall commitment to diversity. Sears values diversity and that attitude starts with the Chairman, CEO Arthur Martinez who has been CEO of the Minority Business Suppliers.
- Company-wide representation of women in retailing averages 52.5%, while 17% of officials and managers are minority persons

215

and 49.5% are women. This compares to 13.9% minority officials and managers and 50.5% women officials and managers in the retail industry overall. Sears also has a program of commitment to vendor diversity. example, 20% of all business will be given to minority and women entrepreneurs.

Toyota Motors
- In response to the changing demographics of its workforce and consumer base, Toyota has undertaken comprehensive diversity efforts.
- "Toyota's diversity initiatives are all-encompassing." Says Barbara Arnold, Toyota Sales Manager.

[Source: Online Magazine, Hemisphere Report, Hemisphere, Inc., www.hemnet.com]

CHAPTER 19: TECHNOLOGY

WOW! Women are now the fastest growing segment of Internet users. Most estimates are that women today are now 48% of Internet users. In fact, by the year 2000 women will make up 50% of the total online audience and 52% by 2002.

- The Internet has experienced a rapid increase it its number of users. According to IntelliQuest Research, it is estimated that the number of adult individuals online in the U.S. is approximately 79.4 million, with an additional 18.8 million people online in 1999.

WOW! Women are the fastest growing part of future projections for electronic commerce and Electronic Commerce is one of the hottest trends in this nation and the globe. Watch for WOWFactor for example to emerge as the largest electronic commerce site for women.

- Forrester Research estimates that the total goods traded over the web in the U.S. in 1997, reached $ 9 billion. In the year 2000, Forrester expects the total goods traded through electronic commerce to reach $ 160 billion. They project that by the year 2002, electronic commerce will be at $ 327 billion, doubling.

- Online Advertising and Online Shopping: Corporate Spending for online advertising and sponsorships continues to increase. Simba Information estimates that spending online advertising will reach $ 7.1 billion by 2002, as a significantly higher percentage of women and middle-income users visit the Internet.

- Online buyers are spending more over time. In 1998, according to CnetNews.com, 35% of online buyers spend more that $ 300 online. This was an 11% increase from 1997. 1 800 Flowers and others report as do the airlines enormous jumps ahead for electronic purchasing.

Electronic Commerce is Hot:

- 35% of the Internet population, according to a study by Jupiter Communications, has made an online purchase in the past year.

- **E commerce or online shopping revenues will increase 784%** over the next four years according to eMarketer's eCommerce: *Retail Shopping Report.*

- **WOWFactor** is a company engaged in the business of promoting E-commerce through its web site devoted to professional women and women owned businesses. The launch in May, 1999, will host 1.2 million women business owners. It will offer free initially a unique service that allows the user to request a personal, limited search of the business profiled in the WOWFactor directory.

- **Business Women's Network** (BWN), offers the access to information on all the sites for women and has a partnership with WOWFactor.

- **iVillage!** As the largest Web site for women, has an electronic commerce section which has been called iBaby. iVillage! Has several million visitors per month as the largest overall women's web site but electronic commerce is not the largest part of the site.

WOW! **Women business owners are the fastest growing segment of women online,** with a 450% increase projected from 1996 to 2000.

WOW! **79% of women online use e-mail.** We are communicators. Americans send 2.2 billion Email messages per day and only 293 million pieces of first class mail.
[Source: U.S. News and World Report.]

WOW! 70% of women business owners, compared to 10% of male business owners, say the **most important reason for adopting technology is to explore new strategies for growth.**

WOW! **23% of women entrepreneurs have a home page.** This compares to **men at 15%.**

WOW! Women are using the web for business communications more than men. **51% of women now use the Internet for business communications compared to 40% of men.**

WOW! **94% of Business Web sites are used to advertise the company and its products.**
[Source: PriceWaterhouseCoopers]

WOW! **80% of working women believe that technology is a key** contributing factor to their higher salaries. The same percentage views **technological proficiency as the entry into traditionally male-dominated fields.**

219

WOW! FACTS

WOW! Women purchase 66% of all computers.

WOW! 7 out of 10 women in the workplace view technology as a powerful equalizer on the economic playing field between men and women.

WOW! Professional women earning more than $45,000 a year are three times more likely to be frequent computer users. 73% of these professional women say technology is helping them achieve their goals.

WOW! Technology boosts growth in home-based businesses. Most home-based businesses are currently using computers;
- 73% use desktops, 20% use laptops,
- 57% use computer modems.
- 53% have CD-ROM capability.

WOW! 56% of women online are mothers.

WOW! Barnes and Noble's online store **www.barnesandnoble.com** is a popular Web site for women.

220

ACTS

TECHNOLOGY RESOURCES

Examples:

Wired Women, www.wiredwoman.com: A group where women can learn and share ideas about new technology in a comfortable and dynamic space. Training for women and girls in computer technology is offered, as well as networking.

Wow! Factor, wwwfactor.com.: Electronic commerce for women.

WWW Virtual Library for Women, www.nwrc.org/vlwomen.

WWW Women Online, www.women.com: Search directory for women.

Women's Home Page, www.mit.edu: Online resources

Women's Resources, www.sunsite.unc.edu/cherlyb/women/wresources

Electronic   Forms   For   Women:, www.unix.umbc.edu.korenman/wmst/forums

WOW! FACTS™

CHAPTER 20: HEALTH

WOW! Average **life expectancy** for women today is **76 years.**

WOW! **Approximately 9 million women of childbearing age lack health insurance.** Women ages 15-44 have out-of-pocket expenditures for health care services that are 68% higher than such expenditures for men of the same age ($573 vs. $342).

WOW! **58% of the American public fear they may be denied a medical procedure** under their existing medical coverage. **56% say they fear not being able to go to a doctor of their choice.**

WOW! **Women make up the majority of nursing home residents,** living longer than men and having more chronic illnesses.

WOW! The average annual cost of nursing home care in the U.S. is $40,000; the average cost is $80,000+ in the New York metropolitan area.

WOW! **Corporate America is playing an active role in health initiatives, research and treatment for women.** Corporate manufacturers, retailers, and financial institutions are becoming involved – companies such as Johnson & Johnson, Avon, The Limited, Revlon, Eli Lilly, Fannie Mae, Bristol Myers Squibb, and many others. These companies are investing millions of dollars each year for research and support for programs ranging from cancer research to anti-violence initiatives.

MALE AND FEMALE PHYSICIANS

YEAR	MALE		FEMALE	
1996	580,377	78.7%	157,387	21.3%
1995	358,106	90.9%	350,636	9.1%
1990	511,227	83.1%	104,194	16.9%
1985	471,991	85.4%	80,725	14.6%
1980	413,395	88.4%	54,284	11.6%

HEART DISEASE

WOW! Each year in the United States more than 1.5 million people will suffer heart attacks. Of these, two-thirds will survive.

WOW! One in four American adults have high blood pressure. The good news is that many can prevent it, and others can control it.

WOW! Only 31% of women surveyed by the American Heart Association knew that heart disease and stroke were the leading causes of death for women. 50% thought cancer was the leading cause of death.

WOW! Only 18% of women said they saw, heard, or read any information about heart disease in their health care professional's office in the last twelve months.

CANCER

WOW! One in eight women will develop breast cancer at some point in their lives.

WOW! The survival rate for cancer patients is 73% today, almost 50% higher than it was in 1950.

WOW! 23.1 million women in the U.S. smoke, and more than 145,000 women die every year from smoking related diseases.

WOW! In 1999, the U.S. Centers for Disease Control entered into its ninth year of a landmark national program, bringing critical breast and cervical cancer screening services to under-served women. This includes older, low income, underinsured women and minority women.. In addition, The National Cancer Institute created CancerNet for up to date information.

OSTEOPOROSIS

WOW! 80% of the 28 million Americans affected by osteoporosis are women.

WOW! Women are **four times more likely to get osteoporosis** than are men and more than **23 million women are at risk** for developing this disease which makes bones extremely fragile.

225

VIOLENCE AGAINST WOMEN

WOW! 50-80% of women in the U.S. experience some from of sexual harassment during their academic or work lives.

WOW! 102,555 women were victims of rape in 1990. One in three women will be raped during their lifetime.

WOW! 50% of the homeless women and children have been made homeless by violence in the home.

WOW! Battering is the leading cause of injury to women aged 13-44 in the U.S. experience some form of sexual harassment during their academic or

[Source: Doors of Hope/ National Network To End Domestic Violence Fund]

WOW! Domestic violence is **abuse that occurs within an intimate relationship.**

WOW! **Domestic violence is not limited to physical assault.** It can also include emotional, sexual, psychological and economic abuse. Domestic violence may involve coercion, threats, intimidation, harassment, stalking, violence towards pets, property, or actual physical violence.

WOW! **Domestic violence is widespread.** According to the U.S. Surgeon General, **domestic violence is the greatest single cause of injury**

among US women, accounting for more emergency room visits than auto accidents, mugging, and rape combined.

WOW! **Approximately 4 million American women are battered every year.** Battering may start, or become worse, during pregnancy. Once violence begins, it tends to increase over time and become more severe.

WOW! **Two-thirds of abused children are being parented by a battered woman.** Children who witness, and/or are victims of violence, are at a higher risk of becoming the next generation of victims and abusers, for experimenting with drugs and alcohol, for running away from hone and for having problems in school.

WOW! **Domestic violence occurs in families of all races, religions, economic and social backgrounds.** It is not a problem affecting only the poverty-stricken or specific ethnic groups.

HOW CAN A VICTIM OF DOMESTIC VIOLENCE GET HELP?

WOW! **National Domestic Violence Hotline:**
1 (800) 799-SAFE/799-723); 1(800) 787-3224 (TTY for the deaf).
Provides 24 hour, toll free crisis intervention, referrals to local programs and information about domestic violence.

WOW! **Local telephone directories** include domestic violence hotline numbers in emergency listings for emergency shelter, counseling and other services.

227

WOW! Important Web site addresses:

Family Violence Prevention Fund – a national non-profit organization that focuses on domestic violence education, prevention and public policy reform. http://www.fvpf.org.

Family Violence Awareness Page is a Web site devoted to helping fight all forms of family violence. This comprehensive site
provides local, toll free domestic violence hotline numbers and links to other informative Web sites. http://www.famvi.com

SOURCES OF INFORMATION ABOUT DOMESTIC VIOLENCE

The National Network To End Domestic Violence Fund is an education, membership and advocacy organization of statewide domestic violence coalitions. The National Network Fund provides education and training for advocates. For more information, call (202) 543-5566 or visit its Web sit: http://www.nnedv.org.

"Doors of Hope" is a new national initiative for organizations that help victims of domestic abuse. It was launched by Philip Morris in partnership with the National Network to End Domestic Violence Fund. The grant-making program is the nation's largest public-private partnership addressing the issue of domestic violence.

228

CHAPTER 21: HISTORY AND WOMEN

WOW! Many institutions now serve to capture history for women yesterday, today and tomorrow. However, of the some 8,000 museums in the U.S., currently only four have women as their only anchor point.

WOW! **National Women's Hall of Fame, Seneca Falls, New York.**
The paramount event held by the Hall of Fame is the National Honors Ceremony, at which distinguished American women are inducted into the Hall of Fame. (313) 568-8060; www.women.com/news/hall.

WOW! **National Women's Party/Sewall-Belmont House, Washington, DC.** Chosen as an historic women's site by the President's Commission on Women's History, and one of the four millennium projects chosen by Congress. Call (202) 546-1210, or visit their web site at www.natwomansparty.org.

WOW! **National Women's History Project.**
In 1980, the Project was involved in many efforts promoting multi-cultural women's history. They coordinate the women's history network, conduct teacher-training conferences and supply materials through a women's history catalogue. (707) 838-6000; www.nwhp.org/.

WOW! **National Museum of Women's History (NMWH).**
This museum is planned as a permanent facility to be located on the National Mall in Washington, D.C., assuming all final approval. It will "preserve, display, and celebrate the rich, diverse heritage of women and

229

bring it into the cultural main-stream." The Museum has already launched its "virtual museum." The permanent museum will share with millions of Americans and international visitors the traditional and non-traditional achievements of women throughout history. (703) 299-0552; www.nmwh.com.

WOW! National Museum of Women in the Arts (NMWA)

The National Museum of Women in the Arts is an extraordinary, one of its kind, museum. With great appreciation to the chairman of the Board, Wilhemina Holladay, the Museum presents special exhibitions and has a permanent collection supporting women artists. The Library and Research Center (LRC) has a unique collection of more than 8,000 rare books and catalogues on women artists, special collections, including artist libraries, book plates and artist books. (202) 783-5000; www.nwma.org.

WOW! Women In Military Service for America Memorial Foundation, Inc. (WIMSA). The Women's Memorial is located at the ceremonial entrance to Arlington National Cemetery in Arlington, Virginia. It includes exhibits, a theatre, and a register that recognizes the individual stories of women who have served. It honors over 1.8 million women who have served and are currently serving in America's defense. (703) 533-1155. www.womensmemorial.org.

WOW! The Women's Museum: An Institute for the Future. This museum will open October 2000, in Dallas Texas as a place to celebrate women's history and glimpse at the technological possibilities of the 21st Century. Visitors will be able to have hands-on experience with futuristic technology while learning about the past.

230

CHAPTER 22: SPORTS

WOW! 80% of women identified as key leaders in Fortune 500 companies participated in sports during their childhood and self-identified as having been "tomboys."

WOW! Research suggests that girls who participate in sports are more likely to experience academic success and to graduate from high school than those who do not play sports.

WOW! Half of all girls who participate in some kind of sports also experience higher than average levels of self-esteem and less depression.

WOW! Female athletes do better in school compared to non-athletic females. (President's Council on Physical Fitness.)

WOW! Corporate Support: In the past five years, corporate sponsorship of women's sports has more than doubled; rising to $600 million in 1997, from $285 million in 1992.

RESOURCES ON THE WEB

- **Just Sports for Women** www.justwomen.com. Online magazine that focuses on women and sports

231

- **Ladies Professional Golf Association (LPGA)**, (904) 274-6200. LPGA offers golf clubs for teenager girls.

- **National Association for Girls and Women in Sports**, (800) 213-7193.

- **Women's Soccer World**, www.womensoccer.com.
- **Women's Sports Foundation**, www.lifetimetv.com/wosport, (800) 227-3988. A national, non-profit member based organization dedicated to increase the opportunities for women and girls in sports through education, advocacy, recognition and grants.

- **YWCA of the USA**, www.ywca.org , 212-273-7800

WOW! **Exercise**: 78% of women list more exercise as a personal goal yet women struggle with time pressures. The good news is 93% of women say they exercise at least weekly. 60% want more time for active exercise, yet only 26% say they get regular, consistent exercise workouts. (Fitness)

WOW! **Training**: One-on-one training is increasingly popular. Personal coaches are in demand (Conde Nast Sports for Women).

WOW! **Sports gear**: Beginning in 1991, women have outspent men in their purchasing of sports shoes and sports apparel.

WOW! Top 10 Women Athletes

Athlete	Year	Time*
1. Florence Griffith Joyner, USA	1988	10.61 seconds
2. Marlene Ottey, Jamaica	1996	10.74
3. Evelyn Ashford, USA	1984	10.76
4. Irina Privalova, Russia	1994	10.77
5. Dawn Sowell, USA	1989	10.78
6. Marlies Göhr, East Germany	1983	10.81
7. Gail Devers, USA	1992	10.82
8. Gwenn Torrence, USA	1994	10.82
9. Marita Koch, East Germany	1983	10.83
10. Juliet Cuthbert, Jamaica	1992	10.83

*Based on 100 meters *[Source: The Top 10 Book, Russell Ash]*

WOW! Running: In the past decade, women runners have increased 38%. Women want to lost weight and relieve work stress.

WOW! Soccer: Women like it! Among the US amateur players, there are as many girls as boys.

WOW! Hockey: Women are real fans. Women are 45% of National Hockey League attendees.

WOW! Basketball: Women now account for 50% of the $3 billion market for NBA merchandise.

233

WOW! FACTS™

CHAPTER 23: GOVERNMENT

WOW! Government Resources are plentiful!

WOW! The National Women's Business Council (NWBC),
409 Third Street SW, Washington, DC 20024, (202) 205-3850.
The NWBC was created to address barriers and obstacles faced by women.
NWBC was the leader for both Summit '96 and Summit '98 where
prominent women entrepreneurs participated. The Summit presented a
master plan to unify the economic value of women entrepreneurs. The plan
is a result of Summit '98.

WOW! Interagency Committee on Women's Business Enterprise,
Washington, DC, 20502; (202) 205-6673. The Interagency committee is
made up of key federal offices and programs.

- **Council of Economic Advisors** 17th & Pennsylvania Ave., NW
  Washington, DC 20502; (202) 395-5084.

- **U.S. Department of Commerce** Office of Business Liaison 14th and
  Constitution Avenue, NW, Washington, DC 20230; (202) 483-5777.

- **U.S. Department of Health and Human Services,** 200 Independence
  Avenue, SW, Washington, DC 20201; (202) 690-6347

- **U.S. Department of Labor,** Women's Bureau, 200 Constitution Avenue, NW, Washington, DC 20210; (202) 219-6611; http://www.dol.gov/dol/wb/.

- **Office of Enterprise Development,** General Services Administration, 18th and F Streets, NW, Washington, DC 20405; (202) 501-1021; www.gsa.gov/oed.

- **Office of Women's Business Ownership**, U.S. Small Business Administration, 409 Third Street, NW, Washington, DC 20416; (202) 205-6673. www.sba.gov/womeninbusiness.

- **White House Office for Women's Initiatives and Outreach,** Room 15, Old Executive Office Building, Washington, DC 20503; (202) 456-7300, www.whitehouse.gov.

HELPING WOMEN ENTREPRENEURS

WOW! Government agencies are focusing on women business owners and how they may assist entrepreneurial women to get ahead.

WOW! The Small Business Administration (SBA),
SBA Services to Help Women Succeed in Business, 409 Third Street, NW, Washington, DC, 20416, (800) ASK-SBA. Programs include the following:

- **Women's Business Information Centers (WBIC's)** - assistance at nearly 70 centers in 40 states. A joint venture between the U.S. Small Business Administration and private partners, BCIs provides the latest in high-tech hardware, software and telecommunications to help start-up expanding businesses. Additionally, counseling and training is offered.

236

- **Women's Network for Entrepreneurial Training (WNET):** mentoring by successful business women at more than 100 roundtable groups nationwide. Puts together experienced women business owners with women whose businesses are ready to grow. In a year long, one-on-one program, these "seasoned" women entrepreneurs act as mentors (or in this case woman-tors) to their less experienced counterparts (protégés), sharing their knowledge, skills and support. OWBO Director, Sherry Henry says, "The mentors have a wealth of expert knowledge about when to experiment, diversify, expand, conserve, or take risks."

- **Office of Women's Business Ownership (OWBO)** is the only federal government program established to **help women become full partners in economic development** through small **business ownership. They have representatives in each Federal Regional Office across the U.S. Online OWBO also operates the Women's Business Center**—a comprehensive training, counseling, and information resource on the Internet.

- **The National Women's Business Center, Inc. (WBC)** is a non-profit organization in public-private partnership with the OWBO of the SBA.

- **SCORE** provides resources and counseling services online. 25,000 members make up this volunteer program, providing expert advice to present and prospective owners and managers of small businesses. Volunteers come from all fields and all levels of business. (202) 205-7625.

- **Small Business Development Centers**—help entrepreneurs to get started and grow successfully. Promotes economic development by providing a variety of management, business planning, marketing, tax and accounting and financial assistance to current and prospective small business owners. Each center is tailored to the local community and individual client. The staff consists of graduate business students,

237

university faculty, and volunteers from the professional community. (202) 205-6817.

- **One-Stop Capital Shops**—Set up specifically to help businesses in Empowerment Zones and Enterprise Communities.
- **Procurement PRO-Net**—Procurement Network.
- **Women-Owned Small Business Procurement Program.**

SBA LENDING PROGRAMS

Loan Guaranty Program, is one of SBA's primary lending programs. It provides loans to small businesses unable to secure financing on reasonable terms through normal lending channels. The program operates through private-sector lenders that provide loans which are, in turn, guaranteed by the SBA -- the Agency has no funds for direct lending or grants.

WOW! SBA has recently announced a new markets initiative. It creates new financial products and establishes a 'circle of influence' among lenders, entrepreneurs and technical assistance providers.

The New Markets Initiative includes:

- SBALowDoc and SBAExpress: smaller loans up to $150,000 with smaller fees and higher guarantees. The average SVA loan size is $229.000. Current capital efforts focus on investments of $500,000 to $5 million.
- Microlending: doubling the number of lenders.
- Small Business Investment Company expansion.
- New Markets Venture Capital Companies with smaller sized investments.
- Very Small Business Pilot Program, with procurement assistance for firms with fewer than 15 employees and receipts less than $1 million.
- E-commerce support helping small business engage in E-commerce.
- Expanding Women's Business Center Network. Doubling the size and insuring they are in each state for the future.
- 20 new One Stop Capital Shops in Empowerment Zones.

238

SOURCES

The Business Women's Network (BWN) has used more than five hundred different resources in the production of the *WOW! Facts*. We have expended approximately 3,500 hours to identify subject areas, specify who has the best materials, solicit the information, digest and analyze it and produce the *WOW! Facts*. Thanks to all.

Credits are due to the following as a sampling of the best resources:

Abbott Wood Media Marketing and Information Resources
A.C. Nielson
Adelphi University
AFL-CIO - Department of Professional Employees
Alliance of Business Women International
Allstate Insurance
American Association of Retired Persons – Women's Initiative
American Association of University Women
American Association of University Professors
American Business Collaboration for Quality Dependent Care
American Council on Education – Women's Program
American Demographics

American Physical Therapy Association
American Society for Training and Development (ASTD)
American Woman, The
Association of Small Business Development Centers
Association of Women's Business Centers
AT&T
ATHENA Foundation
The Australian Embassy
Avon
Bank Boston
Bank of America
Bankers Trust
Bartos, Rena
Biz Women
Black Enterprise
BPW Foundation
Bright Horizons

239

Bureau of Labor Statistics, U.S. Department of Labor
Business & Professional Women
Business Week Magazine
Business Women's Network
BWN Calendar of Women's Events
BWN Directory, 5th Edition 1998
BWN Diversity Report
Canadian Business Women's Council
Canadian Embassy
Catalyst
Census Bureau
Center for American Women & Politics
Center for Childcare Workforce
Center for Creative Leadership
Center for Policy Alternatives
Center for Women & Enterprise – Boston
Challenger, Gray and Christmas
College and University Personnel
Colorado, State of – Small Business Development
Commerce Department
Commission on the Status of Women
Committee of 200
Conference Board, The
Covenant, The – from the Greater Dallas Chamber of Commerce

Dial-a-Mentor
Dingman Center for Entrepreneurship
Dun & Bradstreet
Education Department Resource Center
Education Research Services
Electronic Resource Center
Entrepreneurial Center, The
Entrepreneur Magazine
Ernst & Young Financial Planning for Women
Executive Female Magazine
Families and Work Institute
Federal Communications Commission
Federal Reserve Board
Financial Women's Association of New York
Forbes Magazine
Global Enterprise Group (GEG)
GovExec
Health & Human Services, US Department of
Heidrick & Struggles
Hemisphere, Inc.
Hispanic Business Magazine
Home Business Magazine
IBM
IDC
Inc. Magazine
Independent Means – Jolene Godfrey
An Income of Her Own

Independent Sector
Institute for Women's Policy Research
Inter-Agency Committee on Women's Business Enterprise
Inter-Agency Council on Women
International Alliance, The
iVillage
U.S. Justice Department
Kauffman Center for Entrepreneurial Leadership
Korn/Ferry International
KPMG
Latina
Labor, US Department of
Leadership America
Lifetime
Maryland, University of
MBE Magazine
Merrill Lynch
Meyers, Gerry
Ms. Foundation
National Association for Female Executives
National Association for Health Care Recruitment
National Association of Home Based Businesses
National Association of Small Business Investment Companies
National Association of the Self-Employed
National Association of Women Business Owners

National Center for Women and Aging/Brandeis University
National Committee for Responsive Philanthropy
National Committee on Pay Equity
National Council of Negro Women
National Education Center for Women in Business – Seton Hill College
National Federation of Business and Professional Women
National Federation of Independent Business
National Foundation of Women Business Owners
National Foundation of Women Legislators
National Network on Women and Philanthropy
National Partnership for Women and Families
National Science Foundation
National Small Business United
National Society of Professional Engineers
National Women's Business Council
National Women's Party
Nation's Business
Newspaper Association of America
New Women New Leadership

241

9to5, National Association of Working Women
Office of Federal Contract Compliance
Paine Webber
Philip Morris
PowerPlay
Presidential Personnel Office, The
Public Relations Society of America
Robert Half International
Roper Starch Worldwide
San Diego State University
SBA Women's Online Center
SBA – Office of Women's Business Owners
SBA – Office on Advocacy
SCORE!
Securities & Exchange Commission
Securities Industry Association
Simmons College Program on Women
Small Business Opportunities
Society of Human Resource Management
Society of Women Engineers
Spencer Stuart
Statistical Handbook on Women in America
365 Days of Women Calendar
Towery, Matt

Treasury, US Department of
Trickle Up Program Inc.
U.S. Census Bureau
U.S. Chamber of Commerce
U.S. Small Business Administration
University of California, Davis
Washington Center, The
WBENC – Women's Business Enterprise National Council
WBOC – Women Business Owners of Canada, Inc.
White House Office of Women's Initiatives & Outreach
White House Project, The
Wired Women
Women Trends
Women Business Enterprise National Council
Women in Business
Women in International Trade
Women in New Growth States (WINGS)
Women in Technology, Inc.
Women in Technology International
Women, Inc.
Women's Bureau – Department of Labor
Women's Business Journal
Women's Campaign Fund
Women's Caucus – U.S. Congress
Womenconnect.com

Women's Exchange
Women's Foreign Policy Group
Women's Funding Network
Women's Health Office – HHS
Women's Leadership Connection
Women's Policy, Inc.
Women's Resource Center of New York, Inc., The
Women's Summit
Women's Web
Women's Wire
Women's World Banking

Women's Yellow Pages – National Association
Work and Family Institute
Working at Home Magazine
Working Mother Magazine
Working Woman Magazine
WOW Factor
Yankelovich Partners
<u>She Works, He Works</u> by Rosalind Barnett and Rivers

243

WOW! FACTS™

INDEX

245

251

The Business Women's Network Presents

The most salient information about the growing women's marketplace containing economic facts that demonstrate how women are making giant strides.

Pricing:

# of Copies	Cost per	Shipping each
1 - 5	$7.95	$2.25
6 - 50	$5.00	
51 - 200	$4.50	please allow 2-3 weeks
201 - 500	$3.75	
501 - and above	$2.50	

DC residents add 5.75% sales tax

Order your copies **NOW!**

Fax this order form to: BWN • Attn: John Petty
202/833-1808 -or- Mail to:
Business Women's Network
1146 19th St., NW • 3rd Floor Washington, DC 20036

Order your copy now!

Yes, I would like to purchase a copy(s) of the **BWN**

Total number of copies_____ x $_____ + Shipping _____
(DC 5.75% sales tax)$_____ = Total $_____

Method of Payment (if by check, make payable to Business Women's Network):
Master Card/Visa/AMX_____ Exp. date_____
Cardholder name:_____
Signature: _____
                                                                (authorization for payment)
Daytime phone:_____ Evening phone:_____
Billing address: _____
City _____ State_____ Zip_____
Send order to:
Company _____
Mr./Ms. _____ Title_____
Address _____
City _____ State_____ Zip_____
Phone _____

BWN *is a Woman-Owned Business*